T0247868

THE GANGS OF ZION

THE GANGS OF ZION

A BLACK COP'S CRUSADE IN MORMON COUNTRY

#1 *New York Times* bestselling author of *Black Klansman*

RON STALLWORTH

with Sofia Quintero

LEGACY
LIT

NEW YORK   BOSTON

Copyright © 2024 by Ron Stallworth

Jacket design by Eli Mock. Jacket photo by Getty Images.
Jacket copyright © 2024 by Hachette Book Group, Inc.

Legacy Lit
Hachette Book Group
1290 Avenue of the Americas
New York, NY 10104
LegacyLitBooks.com
@LegacyLitBooks

First Edition: September 2024

Legacy Lit is an imprint of Grand Central Publishing. The Legacy Lit name and logo are registered trademarks of Hachette Book Group, Inc.

The publisher is not responsible for websites (or their content) that are not owned by the publisher.

The Hachette Speakers Bureau provides a wide range of authors for speaking events. To find out more, go to hachettespeakersbureau.com or email HachetteSpeakers@hbgusa.com.

Legacy Lit books may be purchased in bulk for business, educational, or promotional use. For information, please contact your local bookseller or the Hachette Book Group Special Markets Department at special.markets@hbgusa.com.

Print book interior design by Marie Mundaca

Library of Congress Cataloging-in-Publication Data

Names: Stallworth, Ron, author. | Quintero, Sofia, author.
Title: The gangs of Zion : a Black cop's crusade in Mormon country / Ron Stallworth, with Sofia Quintero.
Description: First edition. | New York : Legacy Lit, [2024]
Identifiers: LCCN 2024014005 | ISBN 9781538765944 (hardcover) | ISBN 9781538765951 (ebook)
Subjects: LCSH: Stallworth, Ron. | Gangs—Utah—Case studies. | African American police—Utah—Case studies. | Police—Utah—Case studies. | Racism—Utah—Case studies.
Classification: LCC HV6439.U7 U878 2024 | DDC 364.106/909792258—dc23/eng/20240516
LC record available at https://lccn.loc.gov/2024014005

ISBNs: 9781538765944 (hardcover), 9781538765951 (ebook)

Printed in Canada

MRQ

Printing 1, 2024

Dedicated to a "Good Cop"
Detective Kevin Crane (1953–2016)
Salt Lake City Police Department (1977–2007)
My partner of five years (1989–94)
My friend of the last thirty-seven years of his life (1989–2016)
We had fun while changing the face of Utah law enforcement.

CONTENTS

INTRODUCTION

The real Ron Stallworth infiltrated a Black radical orga-
nization for 3 years (not for one event like the movie
[BlacKkKlansman] portrays) where he did what all
papers from the FBI's Counter Intelligence program
(Cointelpro) that were found through the freedom of
information act tell us he did—sabotage a Black radical
organization whose intent had to do with at the very least
fighting racist oppression.

This quote is part of a lengthy social media post written by
Raymond Lawrence "Boots" Riley, a lifelong community activist and hip-hop artist turned film director. In August 2018, he
took to Twitter (now known as X) to post a three-page "political
critique of the content and timing of the film" *BlacKkKlansman*,
fellow director Spike Lee's adaptation of my *New York Times*
bestselling memoir *Black Klansman*, and defame me in the
process. Because of the Oscar buzz surrounding the film, that

post went viral and was covered in the major entertainment outlets including *Variety,* the *Hollywood Reporter,* and *Rolling Stone.* Accusing a Black person of being an informant—especially for J. Edgar Hoover's FBI—is a heinous thing to do, and his blatant lie infuriated me.

I inhabit two identities that most people view as contradictory: I am both a Black man and a cop. Because of this alleged paradox, I have often found myself unable to fit fully in either group. Cops did not accept me because I'm Black, and minority communities distrusted me because I was a cop. Yet to me these seemingly incongruous selves made me the perfect person for the Black Klansman investigation in Colorado as well as the anti-gang work I did later in Utah.

In the wake of the studio's campaign for the Academy Awards, virtually everyone associated with making *BlacKkKlansman* asked me not to respond to Booty's essay as it could hurt the film's chance for an Oscar. Although I believed that his jealous intention was to sabotage *BlacKkKlansman* and promote his own film *Sorry to Bother You,* I held my tongue and let his anti-(Black)-cop hatred go unchecked. That is, until I spotted Riley across the room at the 2019 Directors Guild Awards, but more on that later.

As my wife Patsy and I crisscrossed the country for book signings and movie screenings, I was most frequently asked, "What became of you after the Black Klansman investigation ended?" In the eyes of fans, the events depicted in both the book and film were career-defining moments for me. But our personal and professional lives consist of more than one accomplishment, and this well-meaning question overlooks the fact that I had a successful career before and after the Black Klansman investigation where, as the youngest and first Black detective in the history of the Colorado Springs Police Department, I impersonated a white supremacist to infiltrate and undermine the local Ku Klux Klan. I am most known for being the Black Klansman, but despite what some people may think, who I am as a man and as a member of law enforcement encompasses more than that single investigation.

In *The Gangs of Zion*, I will show other tribulations and triumphs that I experienced as the architect and supervisor of a new anti-gang unit in Salt Lake City. I moved to Mormon Country—arguably the most unlikely place for a Black gang cop—in the late 1980s as the popularity of gangsta rap was on its rise and concern over gangs dominated the nation's consciousness. Our new Gang Narcotics Intelligence Unit (later known as the Salt Lake Area Gang Project) had to take on several key institutions in the state that hadn't admitted they had a gang problem. Members of the legislature and even fellow law enforcement could not grasp how a mostly white, Mormon population could be susceptible to the influence of Crips and Bloods. The Church of Latter-Day Saints itself was in denial, attributing the involvement of Mormons in the gang lifestyle to the moral failings of their race or culture. In this book, you will see that I once again found myself in an uphill battle as a Black cop serving a mostly white population. I had to convince major factions of Utah society to accept what I and other law enforcement officers around the nation already knew: Members of Los

Angeles Crips and Bloods gangs were infiltrating the state in increasing numbers and importing drugs and violence into the community.

I also discovered what few others had noticed: that the appeal of gangsta rap to young individuals—the frustration over inequity expressed in its lyrics—transcended race and culture. I embarked on a deep, ongoing inquiry into gangsta rap and came to understand these kids: where they came from, what motivated them, which gang they supported, and more.

Volumes have been (and continue to be) written on hip-hop culture and its cultural significance, the sociology of gangs, and the role they play in Black communities in the context of American history. Throughout this book, in addition to my story, I share a bit of the extensive knowledge I acquired in my commitment to learn as much as I could about hip-hop as it pertained to my objectives as a police officer. Facing the repercussions of bringing the gang issue to the forefront of law enforcement consciousness, I saw the world through the same lens as the rappers I studied and understood why the kids began to value music like "Fuck tha Police."

The more I learned, the more determined I became to share my discoveries with the Mormon Church, elected officials, and my law enforcement colleagues—with the hope that we could respond appropriately to the increasing threat before it was too late, and gangs cemented their presence in Utah and across the nation. The songs were so ingrained in my psyche that when presenting my findings from gangsta rap music to colleagues, I would spit pure lyrics. Then I would break down what each lyric meant and how it correlated to the gang life that we were investigating. The music gave me a clear idea of the motives and principles of gang members and helped me to be a better cop to a community that needed help. I delivered numerous intelligence reports and expert testimonies about the growing gang violence and drug distribution spreading across Utah and the US as an expert on gangsta rap and gang lifestyle—a title that others gave me. People began to contact me seeking my insight beyond Utah.

Ultimately I made my way to Congress. What followed was similar to the classic Jimmy Stewart film, except the ending of *Mr. Stallworth Goes to Washington* is less triumphant. My choice to ring the alarm about the growth of gang life and its influence on our youth on a national stage jeopardized my position at the Utah Department of Public Safety.

Eventually I was called to give expert testimony on a major legal case that captured the essence of the culture wars of the 1990s when an act on a Texas highway led to a civil lawsuit that effectively put rap music on trial.

I wrote *The Gangs of Zion* not only to recount my experience of policing in a highly unusual context during a pivotal cultural moment but also to inform the Booty Rileys of the world that I am a cop who understands American history, is protective of his race, and takes unwavering stands for civil and constitutional rights for all people.

Throughout my tenure in Utah and career overall, I often met people who could not come to terms with the fact that I was a Black man in law enforcement who could uphold the values of both my cultural identity and my professional role simultaneously. The long-standing mistrust of law enforcement in minority communities exists for good reason, and understandably I faced accusations of being pro-cop at the expense of fellow Black people and other racial minorities. The truth is, I was not just one thing. No one is ever just one thing.

In this book, my objective is to set aside this silly human preoccupation with identity to do the right thing. Throughout my time in Utah, few people were able to recognize the complexity of the gang situation. How could a Polynesian man be a Crip and a Mormon? How could someone overstep the boundaries of his role but still do his job in the best way possible? How could crass rap be the intellectual key to understanding gangs and putting a stop to violence? When you fail to appreciate nuance, refuse to step away from your preconceived notions, bad things happen. This is what transpired in Utah, but not without my effort to try and change the outcome.

In addition to my thirty-two-year career in law enforcement, writing is another way in which I speak truth to power. The position I took in the '90s on gang life remains relevant to today's discussions of law enforcement and racial justice, including (to mention only a few topics) police violence against Black people, the proliferation of private prisons, the adultification of young people for the purpose of incarceration, and white supremacy as it presently grasps for traction in all aspects of our society. I hope *The Gangs of Zion* can contribute to these urgent discussions, and I look forward to being in dialogue with you about forging solutions together.

CHAPTER 1:

THE ACCIDENTAL POLICEMAN

While in the first grade in El Paso, I began slacking in my reading assignments. My teacher Estella Levy—I will never forget her, bless her heart—pulled me aside. "You have a natural talent for reading and writing," she said. "Why are you not living up to that talent?" Her tone was tender, and I just shrugged and began crying.

Miss Levy said, "Do you realize that not too long ago, your ancestors would have killed to be where you are right now—in a classroom learning to read and write? And do you realize that if those same ancestors had been in a classroom learning to read and write, they would have been killed for doing so? You have such an advantage, but you're not fulfilling the potential of what those people lived for and died trying to accomplish."

I never again faltered in my reading and writing assignments, and to this day I still hear Miss Levy's voice in my mind.
I became an avid reader, especially of American history. I particularly loved the story of the Founding Fathers.

When I was around ten, I saw the 1955 *Jet* article about the
death of Emmett Till. Comedian Redd Foxx described the magazine as "the Negro bible," and it became nationally known for its
coverage of the brutal torture and lynching of the fourteen-year-
old African American boy in Drew, Mississippi, after a white
woman accused him of flirting with her. As I looked at the photo-
graphs, my mother told me how she remembered the crowds of
people who lined up at the church to file past his casket.

"Did you go?" I asked.

"No, my mother wouldn't allow me to."

But that picture of Emmett Till in his casket stuck in my head
all those years, the first image of white supremacy and the depths
of its brutality, awakening an awareness in me. Prior to that, I
spoke out if I felt something was wrong and accepted the consequences, but I wasn't raising chaos in the streets, participating in
riots, and all that. When all hell was breaking loose in Georgia,
Mississippi, and other parts of the Deep South during the Civil
Rights Movement, we did not have riots in racially mellow El
Paso. I would watch those events as they unfolded on the evening
news like any other TV show. Such militancy was foreign to me.

Then during high school, I discovered that most of the
Founding Fathers including Thomas Jefferson owned slaves,
and perhaps that is where the dichotomy occurred. I remained
an avid fan of American history and still loved reading the

stories about the founding of this nation. But I started educating myself, the love now including uncovering the associated bullshit the Founding Fathers never taught their slaves!

My self-education included watching the 1963 March on Washington where Dr. Martin Luther King gave his "I Have a Dream" speech, and it inspired me. But then I saw the use of fire hoses and police dogs on peaceful demonstrators in Birmingham, Alabama, on the orders of the commissioner of public safety and staunch segregationist Bull Connor. *What's wrong with these stupid Negroes to allow somebody to treat them like that?* I thought. Living in El Paso, I did not witness the racist backlash directly. In my arrogant mind, there was no way I could be a part of Dr. King's army, because I didn't believe in his turn-the-other-cheek philosophy or in protesting nonviolently. *The Autobiography of Malcolm X* also had opened my eyes, and I gravitated toward Malcolm's perspective, though I would not have become a Muslim because I like pork too much.

I also read about Huey P. Newton and the Black Panther Party and admired the way they stood up to the status quo. In compliance with the laws of California at that time, they openly carried guns and scared the hell out of then governor Ronald Reagan. (This is why today California has some of the strictest gun laws in this country—because a bunch of wild Black dudes marched on the capital wearing black leather and carrying guns. They weren't loaded, but Reagan didn't know that.) The Black Panthers put on a show to accomplish their objective, and discovering them contributed to my political awakening.

In the summer of 1972, my mother went to visit my aunt who

was married to an army soldier stationed in Fort Carson, Colorado. When she returned two weeks later, she immediately announced to my two brothers and me that we were moving to Colorado Springs. I was nineteen at the time and working for the El Paso Department of Parks and Recreation. Still trying to find my niche in life, so to speak, I wasn't happy about moving because El Paso was all I knew. The weather was mild there, and I hated the cold. But my mother said, "We're moving," and I had nowhere else to go.

Before leaving for Colorado Springs, I asked my aunt what kind of city jobs were available. She checked into it and told me that the qualifying tests for the police department were taking place that November. If I just showed up at such and such a time, I could take the test and apply. So approximately a month before my mother left El Paso, I moved first to Colorado Springs in time to take the test for the police cadet program. The program was for seventeen- to nineteen-year-old high school graduates who desired a career in law enforcement and was designed to boost minority recruitment although it never lived up to that objective. Applicants had to pass with the same scores required of aspiring police officers.

Once you were hired as a police cadet, you worked with the police department as civilian support personnel. You wore a brown uniform but had the same badge that the officers wore except yours read CADET instead of PATROLMAN or DETECTIVE. Because of your age, you did not carry a gun, but in essence, you were a police officer in training.

I was told in my interview with the Colorado Springs Police Department that I was being hired as a police cadet specifically to integrate the department and inch the needle on minority representation. At the time there were no Black officers, as Black people had reservations about joining the police force. In fact, I had many Black people tell me that being a cop was viewed as being a traitor to the race, but my attitude was, *Fuck you. I don't need your opinion about what my ambition or goal should be.*

To get on the cadet list, I had to interview with the city personnel manager, the deputy chief of police, and the captain of uniformed patrol before I got sworn in by the mayor. I was hired along with a Hispanic kid named Ralph Sanchez, who wore a suit and tie to the inauguration ceremony. I hate ties and refuse to wear them unless absolutely necessary, so instead I showed up wearing a sweater, a dress shirt, and a pair of slacks that my mother bought. You might say that outfit was my first protest as a law enforcement professional. When you turned twenty-one, they transferred you from cadet to patrolman, gave you a gun, and assigned you to a training officer. Then you began training for fieldwork, which lasted for four months.

My decision to enroll in the police cadet program had nothing to do with changing society or making life better for others or any shit like that. I joined the department because I wanted to earn enough money to put myself through college with the goal of becoming a high school PE teacher. The police department simply offered a good economic opportunity. Minimum wage in El Paso was $1.60 per hour whereas I made $5.25 an hour as a police cadet in Colorado Springs.

Whether I would have made a different choice if I had other economic opportunities, I'll never know.

CHAPTER 2:

WE AIN'T BROTHERS

I stuck with police work because I was having too much fun. Every day on the job was different, exposing me to new situations, allowing me to interact with a variety of people, and requiring me to think quickly on my feet. I enjoyed coming to work knowing that the only thing I could expect was that this day would be nothing like the day before.

When I was still a cadet, a Black kid got arrested. His name was Flip Small, and at the age of fifteen he already was one of the biggest burglars and thieves in Colorado Springs. Flip was no damn good, his brother Ricky Adams was the same, their mother was an alcoholic...this was a very dysfunctional family. I was interacting with the jailer the night they arrested Flip, and when he saw me, he asked me to come over to his cell. Flip told me his version of what had happened during his arrest.

"The cop hit me and smashed my head against the car!" he said. I saw no cuts or bruises on Flip, but I thought, *That's not right. That shouldn't have happened.*

I went back to the jailer who was a good friend of mine—an old-time cop named McClinton—and asked him to explain to me why they would beat up this guy during his arrest. McClinton smiled and pulled me aside. "You have got to be very careful, Ron, when listening to what people tell you," he said. "They're going to take advantage of the fact that you're Black. They're going to try to persuade you to come to their side of the aisle, so to speak." He explained that when the cops brought someone in for booking, they checked them for cuts, bruises, and the like and took pictures. McClinton showed me the pictures they took of Flip when he was booked, and there were no bruises on his body. "He's telling you a story that there's no evidence ever happened," said McClinton. "Just be very careful."

I went back to Flip in the cell and asked him to repeat his story. When he was done, I said, "How come you don't have any marks on you?"

Flip looked at me and gave me the Black Power sign. "Brother, you know how they are with us," he said. "Always trying to separate us and everything..."

"Don't ever call me your brother because we ain't brothers," I said. "We got no connection whatsoever."

This attitude was something I had to deal with early as one of the only Black officers in the department at that time. I would encounter people during drug deals who would try to hit me with the Black Power solidarity thing, but I wasn't buying it. When I asked those who were selling dope why they didn't get a job, they would say to me, "I don't want to make slave wages. Why would I want to do that when I can deal and make *this* type of money?"

"How can you in good faith be doing this and look down upon having an honest nine-to-five like I got?" I said, "How can *you* give me the Black Power sign?"

It was *brother* this and *brother* that, and I always resented being called brother by some Black criminal in the street. We had no connection. You're trying to destroy the race. I'm doing what I can to uplift it. When I decided to continue with a career in law enforcement, this would become my theme.

However, it would not be long before I learned that my intention would attract opposition from numerous, unexpected places. Law enforcement prides itself on being a brotherhood, constantly invoking the rhetoric of a fraternity. Yet early in my career I would discover that I could not presume brotherhood from my superiors or colleagues on the force any more than I could a Black lawbreaker on the street.

I was still a rookie in uniform when a raging apartment fire broke out in a three-story apartment building. I happened to be on the other side of the district and had to rush after the red lights and sirens to respond. When I arrived and began to run up the stairs, a detective was coming down, carrying a six-month-old baby. "Go to your right then through the doors," he said as I ran past him. "The mother is still in there."

I found the woman and managed to lift her over my

shoulder. As I was carrying her out of the apartment, however, the smoke immediately affected me. I got down into a duck-walk where the air pocket was, made it to the doorway, and succeeded in bringing the mother down the stairway and out of the building. Once we reached the open air, they put oxygen masks on both of us.

Back at the department, the lieutenant on duty asked me what happened. After I'd described what both the detective and I had done, he asked me to write up the report. "We're going to put him in for the Medal of Valor," he said of the detective.

This was the first Medal of Valor the department was going to award, and the detective in question was highly regarded by the administration. They wanted to promote him to sergeant and felt that having the Medal of Valor on his sheet would give him an edge over all the other applicants. But they didn't want me—a rookie—tainting his chances by getting the same award.

As I wrote the report, I kept thinking, *Can't you see that this is not right?* But this was my first year in the department, and as a rookie I could be fired without cause. Despite knowing what they intended to do, I reported the facts—including that "Patrolman Stallworth did the exact same thing as the detective had only minutes later"—but otherwise I kept my mouth shut. Several months later, the department held a ceremony to award the detective the Medal of Valor and gave me an honorable mention.

I didn't bother to attend, and to this day it still pisses me off.

But that experience also gave me a reality check about what

to focus on. As I advanced from cadet to patrolman, I began to understand the behind-the-scenes politics of policing. I learned not to care about departmental awards. They were not that important. What was important to me was that I'd saved a mother's life and reunited her with her child. That was the kind of officer that I wanted to be.

CHAPTER 3:

STRAIGHT OUTTA COLORADO

I was a nineteen-year-old cadet in uniform when I decided I wanted to become an undercover cop. The notion first hit while I was working in the records bureau on the first floor of the Colorado Springs Police Department. These long-haired hippies would come upstairs, approach the front desk, and ask me for the files on the subjects of their investigations. They were narcotics detectives working undercover operations, and as I recounted in *Black Klansman*, I immediately wanted to become one of them. I began preparing myself for the day an opportunity might present itself, developing relationships with undercover cops, having ongoing, detailed conversations about the work they did, and making my aspirations known every chance I had.

On June 18, 1974—my twenty-first birthday—I was sworn

officially as a patrolman. I also made history as the first Black graduate of the police cadet program. According to departmental rules, I still had at minimum two more years in uniform before I could join the narcotics unit. But only ten months after I became a patrolman, Sergeant Arthur Dalton asked for my help with a unique undercover assignment: attend a speech by Black Panther leader Stokely Carmichael. Because of his reputation, the department wanted to monitor Stokely Carmichael to determine if they should prepare for a possible "uprising" in the Black community due to his rhetoric. This surveillance fell under the purview of narcotics because it was the only unit in the department that had undercover officers.

Except none of them were Black.

As I recounted in *Black Klansman,* I accepted the assignment, received a crash course in undercover work, and headed to the Black nightclub hosting Stokely's speech wearing my *Saturday Night Fever* finest. My first plainclothes experience was exhilarating. Not only was Stokely a mesmerizing presence, but my undercover career was under way and ahead of the usual schedule.

I learned about my pending assignment to the narcotics unit in the men's room at the station. Chief of Detectives Carl Petry happened to be at the urinal beside me when he said, "You want to be a narc, Stallworth?" He had to authorize all assignments to the detective division, so his question meant that the decision to reassign me had already been made. Three months later, in August 1975, I realized my goal of joining the narcotics unit and became the first Black and the youngest detective in the history of the Colorado Springs Police Department.

Being the "first" anything for a minority is always challenging. There's never a shortage of naysayers who falsely believe you were given a step up the ladder based solely on your minority status and who will never accept the legitimacy of your presence. Standing out in the crowd and always on display, you must be prepared to dispel all challengers to your position, perform at the highest level, and reach above and beyond to maintain your status quo. It's an unfair, never-ending process yet the ongoing reality of being a minority in America.

"Why'd they decide to put *you* on narcotics?" One naysayer happened to be Ralph Sanchez, the Hispanic kid who'd enrolled in the cadet program at the same time I had. Being older than I was, he graduated six months ahead of me and foolishly concluded that this somehow meant he was better than me. "What's special about you?" Sanchez asked. While I won't say they were widespread, I heard other people make similar comments. My assignment to narcotics was an undeniable point of discussion.

I wasn't put in narcotics because I was exceptional. I was put in narcotics because they needed a Black face to penetrate Black environments. That said, I was assigned to the detective division after only fourteen months as a patrolman because my enthusiasm for undercover work impressed those with the power to make such decisions. The department broke its own rules when it assigned me to the narcotics unit because I was able and willing to do the work that nobody else could or would do.

I understood that once I got into narcotics, I would have to prove myself in order to continue to advance in the department. Failure is never an option for the first, and nothing short of excellence was an option for me. After two years working undercover narcotics, I had the confidence to take on the Black Klansman investigation in 1979.

Also at this time, I met Michelle "Micki" Zanders in a history class during one of several stints in college. Stylish and warm, she was the type of person who from the first meeting made you feel as if you had known her your entire life. While others might greet you with a simple hello or handshake, Micki disarmed you with a hug, and when you parted ways, she followed up with another. When we began dating, I conveyed to Micki that if she was going to be with me, she had to expect that I would move wherever the opportunity to achieve my professional goal of being an undercover cop led me. She fully supported my career ambitions, and after five years together, we were married in the chapel at the Peterson Air Force Base in Colorado Springs in May 1979.

(While Spike Lee's film adaptation *BlacKkKlansman* stays close to the events of my life, there are a few creative departures. I did not get romantically involved with a student activist named Patrice during my undercover investigation. Spike Lee invented her character to pay tribute to the Black women revolutionaries of that time.)

Since I was a young boy, I have always felt sure of myself,

and the successful conclusion of that investigation convinced me that I had what it took to forge a lifelong career as an undercover cop. Unlike many of my peers, I had no interest in climbing up the administrative ranks and leaving the front lines. I did not question that I had the potential; I just never had the desire. With multiple undercover investigations under my belt, my goal was to become a federal agent with the Drug Enforcement Administration.

"Stallworth, you're good at your job," said Dalton, who had become a lieutenant. "You should work toward becoming chief of police." His right hand, Sergeant James Lilly, agreed. While most people shoot for that position, being chief of police was never a dream of mine. Nor was I the only officer in the department with ambitions to join the DEA.

Then the rift occurred. The narcotics unit of the Colorado Springs Police Department was part of a larger task force that consisted of personnel from other law enforcement agencies including the sheriff's office and two other local police departments. Dalton led the task force, and a sergeant from the sheriff's office was second in command. The task force took a vote on an issue—I can't remember what the hell it was—and I voted with the sergeant. Nobody tells me what to think. As a fellow Colorado Springs police officer, Dalton and Lilly felt I should have sided with them no matter how I felt about the issue, and they took my vote as a betrayal.

After that vote, Dalton and Lilly's opposition to my goal grew more strident. "That's stupid," Dalton would say.

Lilly added, "Nobody should be a career narcotics agent."

I never expected my simple aspirations to be met with such vitriol by those I'd once called my mentors, especially when I had peers with the same ambitions. In fact, the officer referred to as Jimmy in the film *BlacKkKlansman* applied to the DEA at the same time I did. (He eventually left CSPD to become a DEA agent until he retired from law enforcement then went to work for the US ambassador to El Salvador.) But I was the only one who was told my ambition was stupid.

Dalton pulled out his badge and laid it on his desk. "What color is this badge, Stallworth?" Lilly stood nearby, smiling with the awareness of where this exchange was headed.

"Gold," I responded respectfully.

"And now take out your badge." I complied. "What color is yours?"

"Silver," I said, catching on to this shtick meant to put dissenters in their place.

"That's why you do what *we* say."

Dalton and Lilly only had to pull that on me once for me to get the message. Because I was a good cop, they did not want me to leave the department or to advance on my own terms. The fact that they thought they could dictate what I did with my career and could never provide a valid reason why I couldn't remain an undercover cop royally pissed me off.

In addition to them being authoritarians who did not like to be challenged, another factor in my conflict with Dalton and Lilly was police culture itself. The belief is that you cannot be promoted to the rank of sergeant without a variety of experience, and two years on any assignment is more than enough.

They expect an officer to put in some time in one line of police work and then transfer to another, and so on. Meanwhile, they had already bucked their own protocols when they assigned me to narcotics because I had not completed two years as a uniformed patrolman.

I made it clear: I did not want to transfer anywhere. I enjoyed my work in narcotics, got along with all my colleagues, and wanted to stay there. Furthermore, the officer who trained me in narcotics had himself been on that assignment for almost eight years, and no one ever said to him, *You've put in too much time here. Go someplace else.*

Despite Dalton and Lilly's attempts to dissuade me from that goal, I politely challenged their insistence and submitted my application to the Drug Enforcement Administration. The application process required several interviews and a background check. After my interview, I provided the name of an officer to serve as my reference, but—unaware of the politics behind my decision to leave CSPD—the DEA agent approached Dalton and Lilly for an assessment unbeknownst to me. When they heard I had defied their authority and applied to the DEA, they were furious. Eventually, the DEA passed on my application because I had not completed two years of college, but later I would discover that Dalton and Lilly had enlisted a by now retired Chief Petry to tell the agent conducting the background check that I was a good cop but had crazy ideas in my head about being a DEA agent. As far as they were concerned, just wanting to work for the DEA was outlandish, and they succeeded in blocking me from serious consideration.

I continued to apply for opportunities outside of the state to work narcotics, including jobs in Iowa and Ohio. Then agencies began to recruit me. The Kansas Bureau of Investigation invited me to interview, so I made the seven-and-a-half-hour drive to Topeka. After our conversation, they gave me a tour of their impound lot. "Pick one," they said, pointing to the assortment of late-model cars they had seized. "We'll have it detailed for you."

"I'll take the red one."

"We'll have it ready for you when you get here next month."

I made a verbal commitment to the KBI, got back in my yellow Nissan, and drove back to Colorado Springs. Once home I had second thoughts. As much as I wanted to leave CSPD, the thought of living in Kansas did not thrill me: tornadoes. I eventually rescinded my acceptance.

Then the director of the Mississippi Bureau of Narcotics in Jackson contacted me to invite me to an interview. I made the trip, and a few days later he offered me a job. When I told my mother, she was terrified about my moving to Mississippi. Micki and I gave it much thought, and I decided that living in the Deep South was not for us, and I declined the offer.

In the interim, Dalton and Lilly were not done interfering with my career. The attorney general for Colorado had an organized crime strike force that recruited officers from all over the state. He already had an officer from Colorado Springs, wanted to add one more, and specifically requested me. The colleague who was already on the task force made me aware of what was occurring behind the scenes: Once again, Dalton and Lilly derailed my opportunity for advancement. "Stallworth is too good of a cop for us to let him go," they told the attorney general. "We need him here." The attorney general never knew that we were in conflict, and instead he hired a good friend of mine—someone whom I had trained in narcotics.

I took my termination papers to the chief of police. "I don't want to leave, but I have no choice," I said. "These guys are doing everything they can to stop me from remaining an undercover cop, and I'm not having it. Are you aware that when the AG's office asked for a second officer from Colorado Springs to join the task force, they wanted me?"

"No, I wasn't," said the chief.

"I was the one they specifically asked for."

"I was never told that."

"Lieutenant Dalton and Sergeant Lilly are out to get me, and their ploy worked," I said. "I can't fight a lieutenant and sergeant and win—they're only going to move up in rank, so I have no alternative but to seek employment elsewhere."

Not once did I say *They're doing this to me because I'm Black*, even when I considered race might be a factor. It was too easy to go down that road, and once you take that route, you can't come back. Racial discrimination may have been the result of their actions, but I believed Dalton and Lilly's primary motivation was control. They were authoritarians who detested being challenged, and they would sabotage anybody and everybody who crossed them for any reason. Rather than accuse them of racial discrimination or even confront them—that was futile—I chose to fight them a different way. They wanted tight control, and I refused to be controlled by them even if it meant removing myself from their authority.

"I don't want anything to do with Dalton and Lilly," I told the chief of police. "Even though I'm happy working here, I would rather leave the department than report to them."

"You're a good cop, Ron, and I want you in my department. What will it take to keep you here?" the chief asked. "If I were to assign you to the strike force, would you stay?"

"You can do that?"

"I can do whatever I think is best for my department," the chief said.

It sounded good but did not resolve the ultimate issue. "I want to be on the strike force, but I want nothing to do with Dalton and Lilly."

"What if I were to allow you to live up in Denver? Work out of the office up there?"

It never occurred to me that a Colorado Springs officer could both live and work in Denver. I thought about it for a second. "I would consider staying under those circumstances."

Now that he had my interest, the chief began to negotiate with me. "I only have one request. If I do this, you have to come down to Colorado Springs at least once or twice a week, interact with the people in the office. Let them know that you're still a part of the department and work with them occasionally on cases," he said. "Otherwise, your assignment will be Denver, and you go live up there."

I talked it over with Micki, she loved that idea, and we happily made the move.

True to his word, the chief of police of Colorado Springs pulled rank on Dalton and Lilly and assigned me to the attorney general's organized crime strike force. I worked a long-term undercover narcotics investigation in Five Points, a largely Black area of Denver that was rampant with drugs. The force was predominantly white and brought me—a new face—from an hour away down the interstate to penetrate that environment.

Over the next nine months, I conducted an investigation that narcotics police refer to as a cold operation. We go into a location where we know drug deals are taking place but we don't know anybody. With no informants to provide access to the criminal networks, my objective was to ingratiate myself with the local populace, build connections, and make as many street-level buys as I could. The investigation advanced as I gained the street sellers' confidence, sought to buy greater quantities and varieties of drugs, and got access to higher-level dealers. The ultimate goal of such a long-term bootstrap operation is to get as many drug dealers off the street as possible.

When you go undercover, you have to create a cover story that you can live out in a way that is believable so that others will buy it. In Five Points, I alternated between two personas. Remember the 1970s sitcom *Welcome Back, Kotter*? One of my personas was Freddy Washington.

The other was Dwight Jefferson. When I was in the sixth grade, I was a sprinter. Once during a qualifying meet in the fifty-yard dash, I was winning my race when—on the verge of crossing the finish line—I stupidly turned my head to see where my competition was. In that split second, Dwight Jefferson sailed past me and came in first. So I used his name for one of my undercover personas. *Hopefully, he'll run across one of these guys I made a dope case against, and they'll beat him the fuck up for beating me in that fifty-yard dash.*

So as Dwight Jefferson or Freddy Washington, I would go into a bar in Five Points, strike up a conversation with someone, and maybe buy them a drink.

"So where you from?"

"Colorado Springs."

"Oh, yeah? What brings you to Denver?"

"I ran into some trouble down there," I would explain. Then I would hint at where I was getting my money. "But I still got a couple girls working for me. One's keeping tabs on everything for me while I lie low up here for a bit."

My cover story as a pimp on the run worked. Unlike the big-city pimpin' you might see on a TV show set in New York City or Chicago, a smart pimp doesn't keep his girls around him. He contacts them by phone and has the johns meet them at prearranged locations. We had a pimp in Colorado Springs with three girls who operated from a pickup truck. I knew a GI who was pimping his wife to make extra money. Anybody can be a pimp.

But as a newcomer to town, everybody did question my story, including the bartender at the bar when I attempted my first buy. I asked him where I could buy drugs, and he asked, "What's your story?" When I told him, he sold me the drink but offered nothing else. Later when I did make my first buy, that bartender watched and waited to see if anyone got arrested. After a few more buys with no arrests, he figured, *This guy's cool. He's safe. And he's got money.* Soon the bartender became an unwitting informant, telling everyone about me until they eventually approached me.

That's how the drug game works.

In nine months, we made about thirty drug cases for various offenses including marijuana, cocaine, heroin, and methamphetamine, and the average prison sentence was three to five years. For my contributions to that investigation, I earned a letter of commendation from the attorney general.

And Dalton and Lilly were pissed off to no end. I kept my promise to the chief of police and reported to the department in Colorado Springs a few times each week, and they resented that I never acknowledged them. If I had no choice but to refer to or interact with them, I never called them "Lieutenant" or "Sergeant"—they were just Dalton and Lilly. With contempt. And because I had the chief of police looking out for me, there was nothing they could do about it.

But I knew that eventually I would have to leave Colorado to advance my career. As I told the chief, Dalton and Lilly would continue to rise up the ranks and acquire more power, and with my determination to remain an undercover cop, I could not avoid them forever. To realize my aspirations, I had to go somewhere they had no influence.

CHAPTER 4:

CANYONS AND COWBOYS

We had lived in Denver for a year when an opportunity came to work with the Arizona Drug Control District (later known as the Arizona Criminal Intelligence System Agency). The idea of moving to Phoenix was very appealing to Micki and me. It would take me away from the cold and snow of Colorado. In Arizona I continued to work narcotics and intelligence and earned my gold badge.

I returned to Colorado to attend a conference and stopped by the police station where I'd once worked. I swaggered up to the now deputy chief Lilly's desk. Without saying hello, I said, "Lilly, I see you've still got a gold badge." Then I pulled out mine. "I've got one, too. Mine says AGENT. I work undercover narcotics as a career." As I walked out of his office, I could hear

Lilly slamming books and cursing my name. That was the last time I ever spoke to him.

Arizona proved to be a highly politicized environment because of a long-standing feud between the Arizona Department of Public Safety and the Arizona Drug Control District that had hired me. DPS was the powerhouse in the state, whereas we were the new kids on the block. Each entity had its officers running around Arizona, seeking to dominate the field of narcotics investigations. Law enforcement organizations throughout the state took sides in the feud. The Arizona Sheriff's Association, which consisted of all the sheriffs in Arizona's fifteen counties, wielded a lot of power and backed us, but the governor threw his weight behind DPS.

A lot of politics were played behind the scenes in an effort to prevent my agency from getting into a pissing war with DPS, but the conflict came to a head during my first year in Arizona. Given the department's long history in the state, my agency had to accept it could never win so we ultimately agreed to change our focus from conducting narcotics investigations to strictly gathering intelligence. The Arizona Drug Control District changed its name to the Arizona Criminal Intelligence System Agency, passing on the intelligence we gathered to other law enforcement agencies instead of ourselves making drug cases. That was when I knew I had to start looking for another job.

Here's how ridiculous the politics in Arizona became.

With the exception of a handful of agents who were paid through the state, my agency operated on federal allocations.

We were told to continue working, but if Congress failed to pass a budget, we had to stop whatever we were doing because technically we were out of a job until it got its act together. "What if we're out in the boondocks when word comes down?" I asked my supervisor. "We're supposed to walk home?"

"Well, get home the best you can, but don't do anything. You won't have any authority. And you definitely cannot drive your vehicle."

This is the biggest bunch of bullshit I ever heard of.

Sure enough, my partner and I were in the desert conducting surveillance on an isolated house when the call came over my car radio. We were on our knees peering through our binoculars when the dispatcher informed us that the federal budget had not passed, and we were out of funding. We were ordered to stop all activity and go home, leaving our vehicles behind.

"Bullshit," I told my partner as I headed to the car. "I'm not walking thirty miles home in the Arizona sun." We waited another three days for Congress to get its head out of its ass and allocate our funding so we could resume our jobs. Those were the politics that made me have enough of Arizona, and I began job hunting again.

In 1982 I received an offer to work as an undercover investigator with the Wyoming attorney general's Division of Criminal Investigation. Micki and I relocated to Cheyenne, Wyoming, where for four years I was the only Black undercover investigator in the whitest state in the country. As the only visible Black presence, I sometimes had to find creative reasons why I was in these towns seeking to buy drugs.

One night I was talking to a woman at a Holiday Inn bar when I noticed a cross-country trucker approaching me. I said to her, "Stay on your toes." The trucker offered me money to "spend time" with the woman.

In other words, because I was a Black man speaking to a white woman at the hotel bar, he had made the racist and false assumption that I was her pimp. But then I thought, *What the hell.* "You can have her for half an hour for fifty dollars," I said.

Drunk and anxious for some action, he gave me the money. I told him to head to a room on the third floor and knock on the door three times. Then I whispered to the woman—herself an undercover cop who was working with me—to go start the car and wait for me. She followed my lead and played the obedient hooker. After I watched the trucker take the hotel elevator to the third floor, I tipped the fifty dollars to the bartender and drove off with my fellow officer.

On another occasion while on assignment in a small Wyoming community, I checked into the motel and decided to explore the area on foot. As I was walking, a beat-up red pickup truck drove past me. Then I suddenly heard the tires screech to a stop behind me. When I turned in the direction of the truck, it was reversing toward me. It came to a halt, and the driver and his companion—two white cowboy-looking wannabes with horseshit caked to their boots—stepped out and approached me with smiles on their faces. "We don't see many of *you* people around in this town," the driver said with his best western movie accent. "What are you doing here?"

"Just passing through and thought I'd stop for the night...

check out your quaint little town," I said, offended by these two "good ol' boys" asking me about my business and referring to me as the insulting *"you* people." I thought to myself, *Am I going to have to shoot these cracker motherfuckers?*

Then I remembered that I had left my gun in my room.

Pointing to a bar down the street, the driver said, "Well, hell, *boy,* why don't you come over to the bar tonight and have a drink with us?" A practice that harks back to US slavery, calling a Black male adult *boy* is one of the most offensive things a white person can say.

Despite bristling at the slur, I said, "I'll see you about 7:00 p.m." The wannabe cowboys got back in the truck and drove away, tires squealing.

At seven o'clock, I arrived at the semi-crowded bar filled with nothing but white wannabe cowboys wearing cowboy hats, blue jeans, and shit-stained boots. An eerie uneasiness came over me as I walked through the door and the white patrons halted their conversations and immediately turned in my direction. (It reminded me of the scene in the film *48 Hours* when Eddie Murphy's character Reggie Hammonds poses as a cop and goes into a country-and-western bar, only to see all the action come to a stop because he's the only Black person on the premises.) Just as quickly as the patrons had focused their attention on me, they reverted to whatever they had been discussing before my arrival.

Toward the back of the bar, I found my two "friends," who had spotted me when I entered and were waving frantically. I made my way to their table where they sat with four other companions, beer bottles collecting on the table. My host introduced me. "We saw this *boy* walking around town and invited him to come have a drink." That was the second time he had called me boy, and I was now determined to make him pay for it.

They offered me a beer, but I expressed my preference for rum and Coke. While waiting for my drink, I casually asked my host if he knew where I could pick up some marijuana.

"Well, hell, *boy*..." That was the third time. "...Joe Bob here has some good weed," he finished, referring to his passenger in the truck. When I asked for a joint to smoke later in my room, Joe Bob (not his real name) gave me a free one and told me he could get me anything else I wanted.

Instead I paid for a round of drinks for the entire table. Midway through the round, however, when I expressed a desire for some cocaine for the road, another one of my new "friends" offered to get some for me and left the table. I ordered another round, and when he returned, he handed me a gram packet of cocaine worth about a hundred dollars. Before the night was through, I'd bought another hundred dollars' worth of methamphetamine from Joe Bob. After a final round of drinks, I thanked my "friends" for their hospitality and headed back to my hotel.

A few weeks later all three men were arrested for possession and sale of drugs. The moral to this story? *Never* call a Black man boy. There could be consequences for your indiscretions.

I was never keen on moving to Wyoming, but that was how determined I was to work undercover. We hadn't even been there a year when I decided I wanted out as quickly as possible.

It's extremely cold. The Black presence is almost nonexistent. I was surrounded by people who loved to kill animals and shoot guns, and I don't like to do either.

In 1984, I heard from a friend I had met while working an investigation in Arizona who went to work for the Narcotics and Liquor Law Enforcement Bureau at the Utah Department of Public Safety. He told me the bureau had openings and encouraged me to apply. "Come take the test," he said. "You can stay with me." Knowing it would stir up trouble, I didn't want my bosses to know what I was doing so I planned an overnight trip. I made the five-hour drive between Cheyenne and Salt Lake City, took the test, and had the interview. I spent the night at my friend's place then returned the next day.

I knew I had interviewed well—I always do—so it was only a question of whether or not I was a fit. I had applied specifically to the narcotics section so I became skeptical when I learned that the Utah Department of Public Safety included the state's highway patrol. "I do not want to wear a uniform," I said.

"We are totally independent of highway patrol," they assured me. "They have their leadership, their own level of supervision, we have ours. We don't mix."

That assurance persuaded me to consider Utah. Upon my return my wife and I discussed the potential move to Salt Lake City, and we did have some concerns. I was aware of the Mormon culture and its conservative nature, but any doubts I had were not enough to dissuade me. I was confident in my ability to get along with all kinds of people and thrive in any environment if I chose to be there.

Micki asked, "What's in Utah besides Mormons?" As my loyal companion, however, she was willing to support me in accomplishing my career goals. She also recognized that the move to Salt Lake City would open more opportunities for her. Cheyenne was a small, overwhelmingly white town of only fifty-five thousand people. Salt Lake City had a population of one hundred thousand, and while predominantly white, it was a metropolitan environment with a more sizable Black presence. This factor would acquire additional weight after the birth of our first son, Brandon, in 1985.

About a week or so later, I received the call. "We want to hire you," they said, "but the state budget's frozen. Hold tight. As soon as the funding's freed up, we'll take it from there."

The budget crunch kept me in a holding pattern for almost two years. By the time I moved to Salt Lake City in 1986, I had lived in Cheyenne, Wyoming, for four years—three more than I wanted to. When I arrived in Utah, I was met again with an absence of Black colleagues on the force, but I was used to that. What was strange to me was the strong influence the Mormon Church had even in law enforcement. But those who know me—which you certainly will by the end of this book—know I thirst for a challenge and am not afraid to butt heads. In fact, I love it.

CHAPTER 5:

ARRIVING IN THE BEEHIVE

So, Ron, will I see you at church this Sunday?" my new colleague asked. He was not the first to attempt to convert me to the Mormon faith upon my joining the force, but he was especially persistent. I had to put an end to this constant recruitment.

Religion and I have never mixed. While I respect others' beliefs (to an extent) and even admire people who have a strong faith, religion is not for me. I especially have no use for organized religion despite having a mother who read the Bible every night for half an hour before bedtime.

"How many times have you read that book?" I once asked.

"I don't know."

"Aren't you bored by it?"

"No."

So I tried reading the Bible, picking it up with the intention to start with Genesis and work my way through it. After five pages, I was bored as hell. The Bible is the most boring book in the world as far as I'm concerned, so I admire people who can study and preach it.

There's too much hypocrisy in the Bible and religion in general for me, and my mother was the biggest hypocrite I knew. She was both a devout believer and a major hell-raiser. Mass on Christmas and Easter were mandatory in our family. Each of us got a new suit for Easter. We went to the church as a family, listened to the bullshit, and then came home for dinner. While my brothers and I were getting ready to go praise the birth or resurrection of Christ, my mother was cussing at us because we'd done something to piss her off.

"How could you be this way?" I said once. "Yet you want us to go to church."

"Damn it, just do what I tell you to do and shut up!"

While I liked getting new clothes and shoes—even though I hate suits and ties—I didn't like the fact that I had to go to church. Then the day came when I had had enough. "I'm not going."

"Yes, you are," my mother said. "You're going to church."

"Mama, you're a hypocrite. You talk about how foul we are and cuss at us all the time, but then you want us to go to church, pretend like we're happy and everything is hunky dory, and praise the Lord," I said. "Well, I don't buy into the crap you believe in. Why are you trying to force it on me? I'm seventeen. If I haven't accepted it by now, I'm never going to accept it."

So I have always thought of religion as a bit of hokey-pokey and snake oil. I believe organized religion is at the root of many wrongs in the world, and things would be much simpler and less messy if you took it out of the equation. Today I occasionally go to church with my wife Patsy out of respect for her, but all I get out of listening to preachers is a good laugh at their antics.

When it came to my zealous colleague, however, I was no longer in the mood to play along with this game. After he delivered his recurring pitch, I said, "I will gladly accompany you to church on two conditions."

Believing he had finally gotten to me, he smiled. "Sure, okay."

"One, if I can date your daughter." That is, his attractive white daughter. His smile faded quickly, and I wasn't finished. "Two, if the Mormon Church resurrects the practice of polygamy so I can have five additional wives. Mine, your daughter, and four more." Although the church abandoned the practice in the late nineteenth century, plural marriage remains a sore topic among Mormons. Since my colleague was flabbergasted, I volunteered an explanation instead of waiting for him to ask why I specifically needed six wives. "One for every day of the week with Sunday being a day of rest."

This white co-worker who, despite the conservative nature of his faith, claimed to have liberal social and political beliefs became visibly upset that I, a Black man, had asked to date his creamy-white daughter. Especially when I used the word *polygamy* and explicitly invoked the Mormon faith as a justification for my condition. After staring coldly at me for a moment, he walked away and never again attempted to convert me.

Navigating the current of Mormon cultural waters became a trivial concern when I discovered that something other than religion was increasing its hold on the state. Soon after my arrival in Utah, I bought about a gram's worth of crack worth $100, one of the first crack buys in the state. Once I had the name of the guy who sold it to me, I continued to investigate. Not only did I trace him back to Southern California, I learned he was a Crip. That information did not surprise me; in preparation for my new position, I had read the intelligence reports that LAPD had shared with Utah law enforcement prior to my arrival and knew there were Bloods and Crips in our midst. As early as June 1987, LAPD had warned DPS that their gangs' members were infiltrating the state.

What did surprise me was how those reports and their warnings were being ignored by my peers. A flood was coming our way, but nothing had changed. Nobody was responding to the threat, so I chose to.

Between the intelligence we had from LAPD (which included a description of the gangs' graffiti) and my continued undercover work to identify key players and their activities, the truth became undeniable: There were Crips and Bloods from Los Angeles in Mormon Country, and they were behind the distribution of crack cocaine in the community. Once away from their territorial homelands, the rival gangs had even formed a unique relationship. Whereas Bloods and Crips were die-hard enemies in California, in Utah they often united to sell crack cocaine for mutual profit.

A particular incident in the summer of 1988 demonstrated

the devastating speed and extent with which the Bloods and Crips influence was seeping into the state's youth. On July 14 of that year, federal agents and campus police raided an apartment rented by University of Utah football player Martel Black. The raid netted 2.2. kilos of cocaine, and five individuals who were affiliated with the Crips were arrested—including Black and teammate Charles Patterson—for suspicion of cocaine possession with intent to distribute. Two of the other suspects hailed from Los Angeles, and police also seized some stolen property and three firearms. After campus police received reports that the suspects were selling cocaine to students in the dorms, they came under investigation for three months. The cocaine purchased by narcotics officers during the operation was tested and found to be as high as 86 percent pure. The charges against Patterson were eventually dropped, but Black pled guilty to selling cocaine.

Only nineteen at the time of his arrest, Black was sentenced to six years in a federal prison in Fort Worth, Texas. In 1984 the fullback had been a member of the Sweetwater team that won the Class 3A title that year, and as a college sophomore, he had led Utah with 253 rushing yards. Recruited from Sweetwater High School in his hometown National City, California, Black claimed he had not become heavily involved in the use or distribution of drugs until he came to Utah, where they were readily available on campus.

As the number of Bloods and Crips in Utah increased, so did the scope of their criminal activity. In the fall of 1987, the Salt Lake metro narcotics unit arrested eight Crips for cocaine sales and another three for auto theft. The following spring, Salt Lake City police arrested a Blood who was barricaded in a crack house with a pound of cocaine. The summer of 1988, police arrested a Crip for distributing a pound of cocaine, half of which had been converted into crack.

During the fall of 1989, the Salt Lake Interdiction Task Force and the Utah Highway Patrol seized thirty-four pounds of cocaine resulting in the arrest of two Crips. The gang problem was getting worse, but the response of Utah law enforcement remained insufficient and reactive.

At the start of my tenure with the Utah Department of Public Safety (DPS), I researched and wrote an intelligence report on the connection between crack and gangs in Utah. I specifically attributed the proliferation of crack cocaine in the state to the emergence of South Central Los Angeles Bloods and Crips in our midst. Because of these gangs' two-year infiltration into Utah—specifically to the cities of Salt Lake City and Ogden—crack arguably had become an epidemic in the state.

The first to document the problem, my report also outlined four steps for a law enforcement response. We had to:

- Recognize the problem, meaning open admission that a Bloods/Crips presence existed within Utah society;
- Educate the Utah law enforcement/criminal justice system and general public on the menace of gangs and how to respond to their presence;
- Establish a central repository of intelligence

information on the problem, using the Salt Lake
City Police Department as the focal point; and

- Attack the problem in its infancy before it took root
  within local communities.

I submitted the report to my direct supervisor and bureau
chief of narcotics James Gillespie—one of the few other Black
men in the Department of Public Safety.

Valuing the insights of my report, Captain Gillespie presented it at the next meeting of the Organized Crime Drug
Enforcement Task Force, which consisted of all the federal
law enforcement officials in the metropolitan Salt Lake City
area. The OCDE board was so impressed with my findings,
they authorized approximately $8K to my agency, DPS, for a
full-scale intelligence investigation into the state's connection
between crack and gangs.

They were also enthusiastic about my recommendation to
establish a multi-jurisdictional task force, which would entail
a collaboration between DPS and the Salt Lake City Police
Department. Prior to my proposal, there had been no effort to
address the gang situation in Utah. Drugs were always the number one priority for law enforcement, but they did not focus on
gangs because they did not believe gangs existed in the state.

If you're a civilian trying to wrap your head around how
law enforcement can recognize that drugs are a problem yet
overlook that gangs or some other criminal organizations are
involved with their distribution, you're going to hurt yourself. It
makes no sense, but that's how law enforcement operates. They

focus on one area, and in this case they were focused on drugs. The fact that gangs increased in the area, and that in particular Crips and Bloods were behind the proliferation of drugs in the community, was not the issue; the issue was the drugs themselves.

The day after the OCDE voted to support my proposals, then Salt Lake City police chief Mike Chabries (who sat on the board and wanted to seize the funding opportunity) announced the formation of a gang–drug task force to address the issues I raised in my intelligence report. Prior to Chabries's announcement, police officers were prohibited from using the word *gangs* in any of their reports. They would call them *community groups, youth groups,* whatever. Anything but what they were—*gangs.* Naturally, it came as a surprise that the police department was suddenly interested in allocating resources toward the examination of gangs and gang violence, but people have done crazier things for money. Chabries assigned two officers to the new task force—Detective Kevin Crane and his sergeant, Mike Fierro.

With the three of us on board, the Gang Narcotics Intelligence Unit (GNIU) became operational on April 1, 1989. Although I would be working with the Salt Lake City Police Department, I technically was not a Salt Lake City police officer. Not having to abide by the department's rules, I fully intended to ignore that ridiculous communication policy and used the word *gangs* every chance I got. If I gave a press conference, I said *gangs.* If I wrote a police report, I wrote *gangs.* Heeding the policy would have interfered with my commitment to addressing the problem of gangs in Utah, so I used the word in every document, interview, or conversation I had. (A little over a year later when we received a federal grant, we renamed ourselves the Salt Lake Area Gang Project. The unit I conceived still exists today as the Metro Gang Unit.)

Little did I know that this moment marked the beginning of an unlikely journey. It would take me from the streets of Salt Lake City to the halls of power in the state, and eventually across the nation and to the capital. And there would be major bumps along the route, some I anticipated, and others I could not have foreseen.

CHAPTER 6:

YOU'RE NOT IN DISNEYLAND

Thirty minutes after we were introduced, Kevin asked me, "Do you believe in God?"

It was our first night as partners in the newly formed GNIU, so I decided to spare him. Carefully choosing my words, I replied, "I believe in a higher being." *But probably only because it was ingrained in me as a child.*

"Do you go to church?"

"The last time I attended a church service that wasn't a wedding or funeral was in 1969."

Kevin smiled, and unlike the other Mormon cops I had encountered before him, he let it go. A few days later, he mentioned that he had served in the air force at Peterson Air Force Base in Colorado Springs circa 1974.

"Oh, yeah? I was a young patrolman with the Colorado

Springs Police Department at that time," I said, amused that
we might have crossed paths earlier in our lives. "I might have
arrested you for being drunk and disorderly."

"No, I'm a Mormon," Kevin quickly reminded me without
a hint of offense. "We don't drink alcohol."

"Never?"

"The only time I have alcohol is when I come down with a
cold and take a dose of Nyquil," he said, shaking his head and
smiling. "It's the closest thing to a buzz I ever get."

Utahns have a reputation for being exceedingly polite,
and law enforcement is no exception. In sharp contrast with
the LAPD, Utah police treated gangs with such softness and
kindness, it was easy for them to do their business. And they
were brazen about it, like a fourteen-year-old Crip whom Kevin
and I busted at the mall for shoplifting. We handcuffed him
and brought him to the security office. As I processed him,
he sneered at the gun on my hip. "Is that a 9mm?" he asked.
Before I could respond, the young Crip said, "We got those.
We got .357s, we got .38s, we got .45s, we got MAC-10s, we got
AK-47s, we got Uzis…And what do you all have? Just a 9mm
and a shotgun. You can't keep up with us."

The kid pissed me off to no end because he was telling the
truth. These gang members looked at us as a joke. Utah was
such fertile ground for them, another Crip told me that coming
to Salt Lake City was like going to Disneyland.

That set me on a mission to change that perception.

So when word on the street got back to me that a PJ Watts
Crip had been bragging that he had kicked my ass, I could not

let it slide. In the gang world, this was a clear sign of disrespect and warranted one of two responses: a physical beatdown or an outright homicide. As a cop, I was legally prohibited from even threatening a civilian with a beatdown. But as a gang expert, I knew that if this Crip got away with disrespecting me—and implicitly Kevin as well—we would have a whole lot of trouble with other gang members. I could not invite the challenges that certainly would come from allowing this Crip's behavior to fly.

Even if standing my ground meant crossing a professional line.

Kevin and I arrived at the PJ Watts Crip's house, and I told him to wait for me in the yard. I knocked on the door, and all six-foot-two and 240 pounds of him answered with a smile. My five-foot-nine and 190-pound self demanded that he step outside and take the ass whipping he had coming for lying about me.

"Aw, Stallworth, I was just jokin'," he said sheepishly.

"That's not how I joke around."

Kevin called from the yard. "Ron, are you sure this is what you want to do?" Neither of us knew how far I'd actually go, but we both understood that I was not allowed to beat him up, Crip or no Crip.

Presuming he had an ally in Kevin, the Crip stepped into the yard. "Yeah, Stallworth, why you so angry, man? Why don't we just forget about it, and you go on about your business?"

"Nope," I said. "You've been telling people you kicked my ass, and now you're going to pay for it."

Although visibly amused by the stunt I was pulling, Kevin

managed to stay in character and play along with my ruse. "What do you want me to do?" he said, putting his hand on the butt of his gun.

I walked over to Kevin as I removed my gun. "Hang on to this for me," I said as I handed my weapon to him. "And under no circumstances are you to intervene."

The Crip slowly approached me as he tried to talk me out of our pending confrontation. "Come on, Stallworth, you know I was just joking." I started circling him, and he mirrored my movement. "Don't be like this, man."

"I'd go easy on him if I were you, Ron," Kevin said.

Realizing that Kevin was not going to intervene, the entreaties of the "big, bad" PJ Watts Crip grew more desperate. "I don't want no problems with you, Stallworth," he said. "I was just talking smack to some friends."

"I don't talk smack," I said, putting up my hands like I was ready to box. When I stole a look at Kevin, who was trying to hold back his laughter, it was all I could do to not laugh myself. "Apologize!" I advanced on the Crip, and he took a couple of steps back. "And don't you ever tell anyone or even imply that you kicked my ass."

"Okay, I'm sorry!"

"If you do, I promise you, I'm going to tell all your boys that you punked out right now."

Now smiling again, the Crip approached me. "We cool now?"

"I'll kick your ass another day," I said.

Kevin and I went back into our car where we had a good

laugh over our performance. Then he asked, "What would you have done if he had called your bluff?"

I thought for a moment. "We will never know." I winked at him, and we cracked up.

As we drove away, I noticed the Crip's roommate standing on the other side of the screen door. He had witnessed everything. Within a couple of weeks, new word on the street was that the Crip was warning his associates not to get on Sergeant Stallworth's bad side because "he's a crazy motherfucker."

Another time we responded to a call about a disturbance in downtown Salt Lake City. Among the families having a casual trip to the local mall, we found a fourteen-year-old Crip and his boys at the food court. When the young Crip saw me, he approached me and bumped his chest against mine. Among gang members, "bumping titties" is a blatant sign of disrespect and a challenge to a fight. All eyes were on us, gang members and families alike.

I smiled at the boy as I leaned in to whisper in his ear, "If you don't take two steps back, I'm going to whoop your ass in front of everyone, and they'll all see what a punk you and your homeboys are." Throughout the face-off, Kevin was standing by me, watching my back and letting me do what was necessary.

The entire time we both kept smiling.

The young Crip glared down at me and then took a few steps back. I shook my head and said, "If you ever step to me like that again, I'm not going to give you the chance to walk away. I will whoop your ass right then and there." Then I added,

"I'll spread the word among my LAPD buddies and Job Corps that you're a punk."

As Kevin and I walked away, I made a parting comment to all the young Crips. "You treat me right, and I'll treat you right," I said. "But if you step to me like he just did, all bets are off."

Most gang members who migrated to Salt Lake City from other parts of the country saw the cops there as afraid to tread on anyone's toes. But this meant that no one was challenging gang violence. I had to change that tune, and Kevin showed me from the start that he had my back. Other cops might have worried about internal affairs, but Kevin and especially I did not. With him by my side, I immediately sent a message to gang members: If they fucked with us, they were the only ones who would lose.

And that went for the organization that was importing the gang members from California to Utah because, as I soon learned, Bloods and Crips weren't serendipitously making their way to Mormon Country. They had a pipeline. A pipeline through a private entity funded by public dollars.

CHAPTER 7:

GANGSTA'S PARADISE

So tell me what gang you're involved in." I never asked them, *Are you a gang member?*; I would tell them. If you ask, you leave the door open for them to say *No*. Besides, by the red jersey and matching bandanna hanging out his back pocket and the hand gestures he flashed to his friend, I knew his affiliation before Kevin and I crossed the park. "Don't lie to me or I'll throw your ass in jail for providing false information to a cop."

Whenever an opportunity presented itself, I still worked undercover and made drug cases if, after assessing the situation, I believed I could pull it off. But my work for the Salt Lake Area Gang Project also entailed gathering intelligence on local gang members and activity, which included significant footwork in public places. We put on our blue Salt Lake Area Gang Project jackets, observed young people wherever they convened, and even approached them to ask a series of questions to determine if they fit the criteria to be added to the gang database.

"West Side Piru," the young man might say.

"So where in Los Angeles are you from?"

"Compton."

"Can I see some ID?" Once I had his name, I would run it by our contacts in Los Angeles and get additional information to add to our database. The young man would hand me a card with his photograph on it, and there it would be yet again. JOB CORPS, CLEARFIELD CENTER.

Founded in 1964, the Job Corps is a federally funded program of the US Department of Labor devoted to increasing the educational and vocational training opportunities for troubled and underprivileged youth. Every year it serves about sixty thousand young people ages sixteen through twenty-four, who enroll to complete their high school education, learn a trade, or accomplish both, obtaining opportunities they otherwise might not have to get ahead in life. Famous alumni include boxer George Foreman and comedian Mike Epps. Today there are 121 Job Corp centers throughout the United States, and they recruit participants beyond their localities and from all over the country. Job Corps is a good program, and I support it…when it's effectively run.

We had two Job Corps in Utah, one in Ogden, and the other in Clearfield. While they were both federally funded, the one located in Clearfield was privately managed by the Management and Training Corporation (MTC). Not only does MTC operate twenty-two Job Corps across the country, during my tenure in Utah, the Clearfield campus was the third largest facility, with a capacity to serve fourteen hundred students; it employed 485 people and had an operating budget of $21 million.

In its quest to help young people find their place in mainstream society—and to rake in money—Clearfield officials unfortunately took an overzealous approach in their enrollment efforts, recruiting from the Los Angeles area, particularly South Central. Many of the kids Clearfield brought to Utah were in or affiliated with the Bloods and Crips who were migrating throughout the United States to open new crack markets. This was how the epidemic spread across the country at that time, and Clearfield's recruitment efforts quickly altered the culture of Utah society with negative and even violent impact.

One Job Corps student recruited from East Los Angeles was Gary Nicolas "Babyface" Avila. He came to the Clearfield Job Corps facility in 1989 and before long formed a gang called Sureños 13 from within the program. The program expelled him, but instead of returning home, he moved to Salt Lake City. Boasting that he was a big bad gang member from East Los Angeles, Babyface amassed a substantial following of youth there who answered to his beck and call. During the summer of 1989, Babyface and his "soldiers" were extremely active in criminal activity including vandalism, shoplifting, burglaries, aggravated robberies, auto thefts, assaults, and drive-by shootings. Sureños 13 quickly grew to be the largest Hispanic gang in the metropolitan Salt Lake City area.

The irony of the Babyface saga is that when Kevin and I

checked with Los Angeles area police authorities, we learned that Babyface was *not* a known person of concern in their gang database. In other words, he was not the "big bad gang member" that he purported to be to Salt Lake City youth. Like the Pied Piper of the fabled fairy tale, Babyface created a false persona as a *"veterano vato loco"* from the LA gang scene to convince naive local youth to dance to his tune and follow his leadership into the gang lifestyle. His assumption of the role of mentor to these impressionable kids who lacked parental guidance was nothing more than a con. Babyface eventually was arrested and convicted in the robbery of a 7-Eleven store but not before he contaminated the Salt Lake City area with his gang mentality and activities, infecting hundreds of innocent lives throughout the community.

The Clearfield Job Corps's introduction of Babyface to the Salt Lake City population created a domino effect of gang violence, and we knew of at least four other gangs we could trace back to its program. Diamond Street, another local Hispanic-Latino gang, was the sworn enemy of the Sureños 13. The rivals turned the west side of Salt Lake City into a virtual war zone with drive-by shootings, stabbings, and eventually bombing each other's homes with Molotov cocktails. By the late 1980s, Diamond Street would be responsible for three homicides.

When I connected the dots between the increasing number of Crips and Bloods from Los Angeles on the streets of Utah and their enrollment in the Job Corps, I followed up with both locations to obtain more information. The Ogden facility was cooperative, but every time I spoke to the staff at the Clearfield campus, a runaround ensued.

"This is Sergeant Stallworth with the Salt Lake Area Gang Project, and I'm calling to verify the enrollment status of one of your students. A Freddy Washington."

"Yes, Freddy is a student here."

"And he's originally from the state of California."

"Yes, Los Angeles."

"And Freddy is Blood-affiliated."

"Oh...no...he's not."

"That's bullshit," I said. "I just spoke to him two days ago in Liberty Park. He told me himself he was a West Side Piru."

"That's not true. I don't know who you're talking to or where you're getting your information, Sergeant. We don't have any gang members here at Clearfield."

It riled me up every time because not only did they have gang members at their facility, but the entire staff from the director to the janitor knew it. As they recruited and enrolled Crips and Bloods from Los Angeles into their programs, they received the same information about them from LAPD that we did. But when we confronted them with the proof and sought their cooperation to address the problem, the Clearfield Job Corps officials doubled down on their lies and insisted there were no gang members on their campus. Meanwhile, they gave these kids weekend passes from the campus, unleashing them to gangbang on the streets of downtown Salt Lake City and Ogden. Throughout the mounting violence, Clearfield Job Corps officials lied adamantly about gang members in their program, denying their contribution to the crime in Salt Lake City so that they could continue to get federal dollars for the program. The irony: Today MTC also runs twenty-three correctional facilities, making it the nation's third largest private prison company.

At one point, the impact of the Clearfield Job Corps's strident recruitment and lax oversight of participants became so dire, it drew local media attention. The *Deseret News* reported that 90 percent of its students hailed from "crime-ridden cities" such as Chicago, Denver, and St. Louis in addition to Los Angeles and cited multiple examples of the consequences of "felon dumping" in Utah, from carjacking to homicide.

I became a regular but uninvited presence at Clearfield, storming into the facility to face off with the director, brandishing undeniable proof that their students were wreaking havoc in the community week after week. No longer able to refute the evidence I had, he switched to another outlandish argument. "They're just doing what any kid normally does when out on the town."

"Except these kids are from LA," I said.

"They're no different than any other high schooler in Salt Lake City."

"Your typical high schooler isn't wearing colors, throwing hand signs, and putting up graffiti. They're not getting into fights over Blood–Crip turf stuff."

"Okay, so maybe they were doing that stuff in LA, but now that they're in Job Corps…"

"I call bullshit," I said. "You're a liar." No matter how many times I confronted him and his staff, nothing changed.

In 1995, I would take my battle against Clearfield's destructiveness to Washington, DC, and learn that gang proliferation through the Job Corps was a problem at centers across the nation. It would not be the first or last time I would speak truth to power in my resolve to fight gangs in Utah and find myself clashing with people who should have been my allies in this mission. In the interim, I found another way to understand the young people involved in this lifestyle that posed as much danger to them as it did to those around them.

CHAPTER 8:

HEADS IN THE SAND

From its inception, the Salt Lake Area Gang Project sought to develop a coordinated anti-gang effort and reached out to law enforcement agencies throughout the county, but I clashed almost immediately with some of their leadership.

Minutes after listening to Peter Hayward, the sheriff of Salt Lake County, at a Rotary Club luncheon blather on about how there were *no* gangs in *his* county, I presented a slide show about the 150 members across twenty-three gangs in his backyard. I displayed pictures of their graffiti and described skirmishes with the police including some of Hayward's own officers. "If there are no gangs in this county," I said, "why do I have reports from *your* deputies documenting their existence?" I turned to face the audience again. "Their crimes are having serious consequences on the safety and welfare of all Utahns, and anyone who suggests otherwise is not to be believed." Hayward gave me an icy stare, and I responded with a wink and a smile. Throughout Utah law enforcement, he was considered a legend; I found him obnoxious.

But at least he never came after my job.

"Ron, why does Joe Ritchie want me to fire you?" When my boss, Commissioner of Public Safety Doug Bodrero, called me, I already knew why. Years before young Black men appeared on the streets of Ogden clad in Blood red and Crips blue, LAPD warned the local authorities that they were headed there for the purpose of dealing drugs and guns. And yes, some of them were students at the nearby Clearfield Job Corps. A reporter from the *Ogden Standard-Examiner* contacted me to ask if there was a gang problem in Ogden. Based on the graffiti tags in the community and the statistics the gang unit collected, I verified that there was a definite gang "presence" there.

To say that there was no gang issue in Ogden would have been a lie, and if I had my way, I would have called it what it was—a gang problem. There is no imaginary threshold where a gang "presence" becomes a gang "problem." Still, while I did not care what others thought when I knew the truth, I sometimes had to play the political game and avoid inflaming the personalities involved.

The next day the reporter ran my interview alongside another one with Chief Ritchie. The headline to mine: "State Gang Investigator Says Gangs in Ogden." Meanwhile, the title to Ritchie's interview in bold letters: "No Gangs in Ogden." Despite my political effort to distinguish between a gang "presence" and a gang "problem," the *Ogden Standard-Examiner* used my interview to portray Chief Ritchie as a liar. Hence, his call to my boss Doug Bodrero.

I explained my choice of words to the commissioner but also asserted that a problem did exist. "I would even challenge the chief to meet me in a public forum," I said. "Put his position on the table next to mine."

Doug chuckled. "Joe has always been…different." Back in September 1982, years before I'd moved to Utah, Ritchie threatened to fire whoever gave a parking ticket to President Ronald Reagan, who'd left his limousine parked overnight in front of a hotel while he was in town stumping for the reelection of Republican candidates Senator Orrin Hatch and Representative Jim Hansen. The ticket and Ritchie's ire made national news. Apparently, the officer who issued the citation to "Ronnie Reagan" executed an impressive forgery of the chief's signature as the citing officer. Calling the ticket a "cheap prank" and telling the news media that the officer was "in danger of losing his or her job," Ritchie ordered the chief of detectives to investigate the matter to find who among his 104-person force wrote it. His reaction prompted an anonymous source to say, *I haven't seen him this mad since all the allegations of teenaged gangs in Ogden.* In other words, years before we would ever meet, Joe Ritchie had been made aware of the "gang presence" in his jurisdiction, and my own arrival to do something about it only fed his anger. "Just watch what you say," Doug advised me.

But Chief Ritchie was so determined to ignore the proliferation of gangs in Ogden, he suppressed the truth about the presence of a major drug dealer in his midst named Willie Wilson Weaver. Originally from San Bernardino, California, Weaver came to Ogden and became a key figure in the Utah Crips cocaine connection. Weaver became known to both state and local narcotics officials during a search of his Ogden residence. A few months earlier, he had been arrested in an adjoining county for the possession of eleven grams of crack, only for his case to be dismissed on a technicality.

Several weeks after the search of Weaver's Ogden residence, police searched an apartment occupied by his stepson and recovered six ounces of cocaine. I interviewed the stepson, and he identified Weaver as the main supplier to a local Crips distribution network. He told me his stepfather received a shipment of one to two kilos of cocaine every two to three weeks, converted it to crack, and then divided the substance among four Crips who sold the drugs throughout the Ogden–Salt Lake City areas. Weaver had been arrested by the DEA in Milwaukee for possession of three kilos of cocaine and one pound of PCP. Between November 1987 and May 1988, he had delivered approximately fifty kilos of cocaine to the Milwaukee area.

In a debriefing that followed his stepson's admission, Weaver himself corroborated picking up shipments of cocaine from his San Bernardino supplier then driving it to Salt Lake City for processing and distribution. He admitted that his supplier paid him approximately $800,000. Eventually, Willie Wilson Weaver received a thirty-year federal sentence.

Yet to the press Ritchie denied the existence of gangs in Ogden and demanded my termination! He was fully aware of the gang–crack connection in his own backyard and had been for some time. Throughout his sixteen-year tenure as chief of police, he never acknowledged the presence of gangs in his jurisdiction even while his own officers were conducting investigations and building cases against LA gang members in Ogden.

One of my responsibilities was training officers throughout the state whose superiors were intent on ignoring or trivializing the growing threat that they encountered each day on the job. In a room full of such officers, I stated that the proliferation of gangs throughout the state was, in part, due to police leaders who buried their heads in the sand and refused to accept the facts. Such people, I said, "were ignorant, dumb asses" who were a "disgrace to their badges." More concerned with their image and reputation than the well-being of the citizens they served, they were fearful that the truth would expose them as frauds and their policies as failures. Though unfair and wrong, I explained to my audience, this preoccupation unfortunately was a natural part of law enforcers' thought process. "These leaders have to divest themselves of the notion that they personally failed," I said. "Acknowledging the gang problem that exists in your communities is neither an admission of failure nor a reflection of weak leadership but rather a recognition of negative forces impacting your communities that must be addressed."

"Sounds like you're describing my chief," said one of the attendees from Price, a town in Central Utah. I had never met Chief of Police Aleck Shilaos. Until he called me the next day.

"I understand that you think that I'm an ignorant dumb ass who is a disgrace to my badge," he yelled into the phone.

"I never said that about you, Chief. Not once did I mention your name. I described a certain attitude by police leadership," I said. "But you must feel a sense of guilt and kinship with my words. Otherwise, why would you take the time to confront me on the subject?"

While he eased up on his aggressive tone, Shilaos refused to back down on the absence of gangs in Price. "Come and see for yourself," he said with utmost confidence. I agreed to visit his city within the next couple of days.

On the day of my visit, I arrived two hours before Shilaos and I were scheduled to meet. Armed with a Polaroid camera, I cruised around town to gauge for myself what was happening with gangs in Price and took a photo of graffiti on a fence—BK spray-painted in blue lettering with a line cutting across the letters. The blue letters signified Crips, who referred to themselves as "Blood killers," the slash implying a crossing-out of their enemies' existence. I also photographed blue graffiti of a Crips hand sign, among other images. But I would discover the most brash visual evidence of a gang presence in Price when I headed to Shilaos's office to meet with him.

Our meeting began with a cordial handshake. He then strongly albeit politely reiterated that his city did not have a problem with gangs. "There aren't even any visible signs of gangs in Price," Shilaos boasted.

"Really?" I said. I could barely contain my glee at the barrage of evidence I unleashed on his unsuspecting soul. As I showed Shilaos the photos I had taken earlier that day, I noted their locations in town.

"I was unaware of these," he said of the images, his tone now mellowed by surprise at what I readily found in plain sight. "How did *you* come across them?"

"They're not hard to find." I reminded him that his own officers were fully aware of the state of gangs in Price and had told me about their activity during my recent training. Then I showed Shilaos the most damning Polaroid I had taken, the exterior wall of a recognizable building.

"Where's this?" he asked.

I pointed to the wall behind Shilaos where he sat in his office. He swiveled in his chair to look at the wall and then turned back to me in confusion. Shilaos stood up from his chair and together we walked out of the building. When we reached the wall facing his office, there staring at us were five-foot-tall blue letters spelling CRIPS and BK with an x painted across them. This wall of graffiti stood directly behind the office of the Price chief of police.

Shilaos was shocked. Every day for God knows how long he'd walked into his office overlooking this visual proof of the presence of gangs in his city. His arrogance came to a halt. Soon I left Price, more than satisfied that I had thwarted Shilaos's plan to intimidate me. In fact, I felt I had accomplished something significant—enlightening a police official about gang activity in his community and hopefully helping make his constituents safer.

A few weeks later, our paths crossed again. I was asked to

serve on the committee that reviewed statewide grant proposals to deal with gangs. As a part of the process to request state funding for anti-gang initiatives, applicants collected signatures from concerned and involved community officials to support their proposals. One proposal submitted by the Carbon School District specifically sought to address the gang problems in Price. When I skimmed over the list of signatories who supported the proposal, I found Chief Aleck Shilaos. The entire time he was publicly denying the existence of gangs in Price, he was simultaneously acknowledging their presence to secure anti-gang funding for one of his school districts.

I called Shilaos to confront him about the discrepancy between his public words and his clandestine support of this proposal. "You cannot deny the presence of gangs and the problems associated with them and then sign a government form requesting public moneys to address the same situation you claim doesn't exist," I said. "That's fraud!"

Shilaos remained silent. I'd caught him in a lie, and he knew it.

"I just want you to know that I know," I said. Then I hung up on him.

I had lost a potential ally, but I confess: Informing him that I was aware of his hypocrisy gave me a perverse sense of pleasure. Yet another authoritarian like Dalton and Lilly who was unaccustomed to someone in my position—a lowly sergeant—daring to challenge what the policy response should be in his city. Like Sheriff Hayward, he was a bully who had run up against someone who refused to be bullied and pushed back.

The denial I faced from the heads of local law enforcement agencies cost Utah. Few jurisdictions received warnings from their peers that gangs were migrating to their area, and the creation of a gang unit by the state's Department of Public Safety should have been a rallying cry for a unified response. As soon as you become aware that Crips and Bloods are roaming the streets of your city, you must respond immediately and vigorously before the problems they create overwhelm you, but Utah law enforcement squandered the heads-up LAPD had given us.

Even when the existence of gangs became impossible to ignore, I continued to experience invalidation. The Salt Lake City Department had sponsored two seminars about gangs where the keynote speakers were renowned gang scholar Dr. Irving Spergel from the University of Chicago and an LAPD sergeant. Despite being the architect of the Salt Lake Area Gang Project, I was not invited to address my colleagues. While knowledgeable about gangs in general, Dr. Spergel and the sergeant each recognized that he was unfamiliar with the unique conditions that impacted Salt Lake City gangs and requested to meet with me prior to his seminar. I spoke with each man for about an hour, providing the same information I had already given to local law enforcement leadership. At both seminars, I sat in the audience and listened along with fifty colleagues as each speaker took the floor and regurgitated the information I had given them—the same information that the Haywards and Shilaos deemed incredible when it came from me. To their credit, both men acknowledged me in their keynotes, affirming the validity of my expertise. My credibility now secured in their eyes, more police leadership begrudgingly heeded my insight from that point forward.

Other people might have been disheartened by the blatant disrespect of their superiors and colleagues, but I kept my focus on the reason I came to Utah. This included furthering my own education toward becoming a more effective gang cop, and that meant opening myself to and immersing myself in topics that most cops would dismiss as irrelevant. To learn all I could about gang culture, it meant embracing hip-hop.

CHAPTER 9:

"TURN UP THE VOLUME!"

What set you claiming, homey?" I asked the sixteen-year-old in front of me. He wore a blue Adidas athletic suit and white Adidas running shoes with blue laces. My partner Kevin Crane and I encountered him and three of his identically clad friends in downtown Salt Lake City. I immediately recognized their outfits as the classic uniform of the LA Crips street gangs. Their hated rivals the Bloods/Piru wore similar clothing in red. The only thing distinguishing these kids from their West Coast counterparts was the fact that they were white.

In fact, we were a mere quarter mile from Temple Square, the world headquarters of the Church of Jesus Christ of Latter-Day Saints, the Mormons. That made their presence even more intriguing to me. "Where you from?" I asked again. While I could not rule out that the kid was a Job Corps recruit,

I expected him to name some location with a Los Angeles area code.

"Orem, Utah," the boys said simultaneously. Kevin and I looked at each other. *Are they messing with us?* Orem is the city next door to Provo, home of Brigham Young University, which is owned by the Mormon Church. A devout member of the church, Kevin shook his head, laughing at the teens.

White kids in a predominantly white and deeply religious landlocked state in the Mountain West acting as if they were Black gangbangers from the urban West Coast. I could not resist asking my next question. "Are you fellows all members of the church?"

Before they could answer, however, Kevin hastily pulled me aside. "The Salt Lake City police are not allowed to question people about their religious persuasion," he whispered.

"Technically, I'm a state employee and not a Salt Lake City police officer," I laughed. "I can ask the question. They're just not required to answer." With a grin on his face, Kevin shook his head, and we walked back to the teens.

"So are you all members of the church?" In Utah, any reference to "the church" is understood to mean the Church of Jesus Christ of Latter-Day Saints. The young men all acknowledged being Mormons, but, more important, they admitted to being affiliated with the Crips street gang. My interest was piqued. "Where are you gangsters learning about Crips?" I asked, barely suppressing a chuckle when I said the word *gangster* while staring at their innocent-looking lily-white faces.

"From the rap music we listen to," said the young man I had first approached.

"What kind of rap?"

The foursome replied in unison. "Gangster rap."

I could no longer stifle my alarm. My knowledge of hip-hop music in general was limited, and I was totally unfamiliar with gangster rap. The genre had burst onto the popular music scene in the late 1970s and soon had the entire country enthralled.

Ten years before this, I was driving down the highway in Colorado Springs when over the car radio I heard, *I said a hip-hop, the hippie to the hip, hop-hop and you don't stop rockin...*

"What the hell is this shit?" I said to myself. My music at the time was Stevie Wonder, the Isley Brothers, the Commodores, and the Jackson Five, but I could not avoid this hip-hop, hippie hip crap. The fifteen-minute version of the Sugarhill Gang's legendary song "Rapper's Delight" played constantly on the radio, disrupting my peace while I was commuting to and from work.

But when these white teenagers mentioned gangster rap, I knew I had to get over my disdain and educate myself. Struck with an instinctive sense that gangster rap would offer a new look into the inner workings of gang life, I recognized my chance to go where no one else in law enforcement had gone and acquire an understanding that few in my field possessed.

When I returned to my office, I immediately contacted an acquaintance named Hourie Taylor, the narcotics and gang lieutenant (and later chief of police) for the Compton Police

Department in California. I described how white Mormon kids were mimicking Crips gang culture because of gangster rap. "Have you ever heard of NWA?" asked Lieutenant Taylor. When I said no, he suggested I listen to a popular album called *Straight Outta Compton*. "Those songs will answer all your questions."

Later that day, I bought the tape at a downtown music store. As soon as I popped it into the car's cassette player, I was captivated by the in-your-face lyrical expression of gangsterism on the song "Gangsta, Gangsta." *Homies all standin' around, just hangin', some dope-dealin', some gang-bangin'.* The song makes no mention of Bloods or Crips.

Then I listened to the down-and-dirty "Fuck tha Police." My first reaction to this bold lyrical attack on my profession was to burst out in laughter. I laughed so hard that I almost had two accidents.

Once I settled down and really absorbed what NWA (aka Niggaz With Attitude) was saying, the world of Crips and Bloods quickly came into focus for me. What on the surface sounded simply like male aggression and posturing proved to be so much more. As I listened very closely to some of these songs, the lyrics laid out information on the intricacies of gang culture: their history, their enemies, their views toward cops and women, and much more. Where everyone else only heard nonsense, I discovered right before me a primer on the inner workings of LA Crips and Bloods.

Straight Outta Compton spurred further study of gang culture through the music, and I became obsessed. In addition to tuning into all the hip-hop stations and TV shows available to me, I subscribed to every hip-hop publication in existence at the time, including *Vibe, XXL,* and *The Source*; bought every book available on the subject—not many at that time; and read any newspaper article I could find on the creative personalities behind the culture. And I fronted all the costs.

I admired the style and approach that rappers brought to their music. They were determined to create it no matter what, and they weren't allowing anybody to dictate how to express themselves. They fashioned an entire industry on their own terms. And I have always respected that aspect of rap music and of gangsta rap in particular. Who would have thought about putting out a song like "Fuck tha Police"? We would not have thought about that back when I was a kid. And that's why I found it so funny the first time I heard it. I couldn't believe the boldness, the daring of going into a recording studio and rapping this stuff.

It appealed to me.

To understand people, you must speak their language or at least comprehend what they are saying. El Paso was dominated by Mexican culture, and we were required to learn Spanish in public school from third grade through sixth grade. After all, we lived so close to the border, you could stumble and land in Mexico. Between growing up in El Paso and my willingness to listen, I learned at a young age the importance of understanding someone's language, whether that language is Spanish or gangster rap.

Before long I had mastered the lyrics to approximately 150 rap songs and was determined to share what I had learned about gang culture with my colleagues. This included the LAPD. "Hey, Ron, have you ever seen or heard of the word *Damu*," a cop in Los Angeles once asked me on a call. "We're seeing DAMU in graffiti here in Los Angeles but don't know what it means."

"In what context are you seeing it?" I asked.

"We see it in red graffiti," he said, "but crossed out with a blue x."

A few days later, I was listening to a song by Snoop Doggy Dogg when suddenly I heard him rapping about killing Damus. Knowing that Snoop was affiliated with the Crips of Long Beach, California, I put two and two together and called back LAPD. "When someone writes Damu, they're referring to Bloods," I explained. "By crossing out their name in blue with their color red, the Crips are invalidating the Bloods." Later I would learn that in Swahili, *Damu* specifically meant "blood warrior." Such knowledge made me the go-to guy for understanding gang culture via rap music, and I dove into the research.

In the 1960s, Sam Cooke made history by providing a gospel of veiled hope for improved race relations in "A Change Is Gonna Come." James Brown, popularizer of funk and a huge crossover artist, created an anthem of pride in "Say It Loud— I'm Black and I'm Proud." But to young Black men and women growing up in what was formerly called the ghetto, Cooke and Brown's approach did not suffice.

As succeeding generations of young people mature, we expect them to rebel. Just as the Black Panthers in Oakland in

1966 encouraged the formation of armed units to patrol neigh-borhoods to challenge white police questioning Black citizens, the gangsta rap movement verbally threatened retaliation for law enforcement corruption, most notably and militantly in the 1988 NWA song "Fuck tha Police." Critics of gangster rap's themes rarely considered either the conditions that inspire such aggressive and unfiltered lyrics, or the fact that the top-ics deemed objectionable are hardly foreign to white culture in this country. Long-standing cultural critic Nelson George made clear in his book *Hip Hop America* that white society's objections to rap lyrics apply to more than just Black kids in the inner cities. "It is essential to understand that the values that underpin so much hip-hop—materialism, brand con-sciousness, gun iconography, anti-intellectualism—are very much byproducts of the larger American culture," he insisted. "Despite the 'dangerous' edge of so much hip-hop culture, all of its most disturbing themes are rooted in this country's dys-functional values. Anti-Semitism, racism, violence and sexism are hardly unique to rap stars but are the most sinister aspects of the national character."

Cultural critic bell hooks also emphasized the sociopo-litical history of Black performers and the inability of certain white audiences to understand and accept what they found as disturbing. "The roots of Black performance art have been the poor and underclass, folks who had to fashion a world of cre-ativity out of what they possess: their voice, their body," said dr. hooks in an interview with hip-hop magazine *Vibe*. "When you take that level of performance art and try to turn it into a commodity, that's trying to reach a more materially privileged body of people—in many cases, that crossover audience of white people—then what can be construed as funny becomes radically different..." She maintained that considerable nuance is often lost during efforts to transpose things considered amusing in traditional Black life to those outside the race.

And with the loss of nuance often comes attempts to censure and even silence. Hence the FBI deemed "Fuck tha Police" so incendiary, it wrote a letter in October 1989 to the record label Priority with accusations of hate speech and a vague threat of censorship. A stinging rebuke by Representative Don Edwards, then chairman of the House Judiciary Committee's subcommittee on civil and constitutional rights charged with monitoring the FBI's treatment of US citizens, halted any further action by the Department of Justice toward NWA. "The FBI should stay out of the business of censorship," Edwards said.

The raw, unbridled fury of "Fuck tha Police" was gangsta rap at its extreme, but the worldwide movement known as hip-hop began as part of the continuum of Black musical expression. Musical icon Quincy Jones certified the validity and power of rap music with the founding of *Vibe* magazine and the production of the 1989 album *Back on the Block*, on which an all-star choir backed up such stellar rappers as Ice-T, Kool Moe Dee, Big Daddy Kane, and Grandmaster Melle Mel. The album's liner notes argued that its intentions were to "share the traditions of the African *griot* storyteller which are continued today by the rappers; the sensuous harmonies within

Brazilian music; the Be-Bop with a dash of Hip-Hop; the power of the gospel choir; the lush vocals of a Zulu chant, a taste of jazz, an a capella celebration—each and all evoking tears and laughter."

Rap lyrics shatter norms in a few ways. They do not always have strong rhyming schemes, and words are often spelled phonetically, rather than the way they are found in dictionaries. Further, the style of speech (once characterized as "Ebonics" and now more widely referred to as African American Vernacular English or AAVE) is removed from what is mainstream and considered generally acceptable. By breaking as many rules as possible in both form and subject, rappers comment upon the otherness of the Black experience in the United States.

Finally, there is a great deal of profanity in hip-hop music. Swear words generally are perceived as an impediment to constructive communication, and vulgarity is presumed to reflect the artist's limited vocabulary and even weak-mindedness. That the strategic use of foul language in art forms such as stand-up comedy reaches across demographics yet provokes criticism when employed by gangsta rappers is, in my opinion, quite telling. In an exchange between Dr. Angela Davis and rap star Ice Cube in the literary journal *Transitions*, the rapper said, "The profanity… we learned it from our parents, from the TV. This isn't something new that just popped up…The language of the streets is the only language I can use to communicate with the streets."

Once hip-hop became co-opted by the entertainment industry, the language of the streets heard in its music became a global phenomenon.

Kevin and I heard the music everywhere. When we went to places and gatherings where gang members congregated, gangsta rap was always playing. If we stopped a car filled with gang members, the music booming from the stereo speakers was always gangster rap. Once Kevin and I stopped a carload of white teenage gang members for a traffic violation in downtown Salt Lake City. They had been cruising State Street, the main location for Friday-night revelers hell-bent on having fun and clashing with rivals. Even as the car stereo blared NWA's "Gangsta, Gangsta," I still could overhear them refer to me several times as a "motherfucker" and "nigger."

The driver nodded in my direction. "Watch this," he told his homeys. Then the driver changed the song to NWA's signature anthem "Fuck tha Police." They all started laughing at me, nodding their heads to the beat while still cursing me.

That is, until I started nodding my head, snapping my fingers to the syncopated rhythm, and rapping the lyrics. Suddenly, they stopped laughing to stare incredulously at this crazy Black cop performing Ice Cube's call to action against the police. Realizing that I was having fun at their expense, their smiles faded, and the driver lowered the volume. "Turn the volume back up!" I insisted. Looking queasy, the kid behind the wheel blared the song again, and I continued, rhyming along with Ice Cube, emphasizing the words "Fuck tha police" by giving them the middle finger. I rapped the entire song while Kevin shook his head, laughing at me as I laughed at them. He eventually returned their identification and sent them on their way. As they drove off, they delivered a final but defeated,

"Fucking cop." Kevin sighed with a smile as we headed back to our car.

Despite our amusement, I did wonder if our encounter had changed the way these white kids thought of gangster rap. At the very least, I hoped that they would reconsider the role Black cops like me played and appreciate the strange position that society puts us in.

As an investigator with the Utah Department of Public Safety, I learned that the acceptance of gangster rap had transcended race. It ironically had crossed over so that white kids, both gang members and those comfortably situated in middle-class suburbia, were now reciting the words to songs that expressed the outrage of living in the inner cities of America. Not only was Mormon Country no exception, but along with embrace of gangster rap came the lure of the lifestyle it graphically depicted.

CHAPTER 10:

"REAL" NIGGAS AND ONE CRAZY MOTHERFUCKER

What's up, my niggas?" The greeting flowed smoothly from the Crip's mouth as he shook hands with his homeboys. These white boys stood yards away from the Joseph Smith Memorial Building in Temple Square where they attended the sacrament meeting every Sunday.

Kevin and I were in the early days of patrolling the streets of Salt Lake City and gathering intelligence on the emerging gang problem, and I'd already had enough of these Mormon kids—and unapologetic gang members—referring to themselves and one another profusely by that word. It didn't matter to me that they were just emulating their Black peers who had migrated from concrete streets to the mountain valley.

Despite my disdain for his language, I knew I had to approach the white Crip with genuine curiosity. "What's a nigga?" I asked. "Define that word."

His homeboys fell silent and looked at one another, wondering how he was going to respond to me. The Crip noted my Salt Lake Area Gang jacket and the sincerity in my voice. "Well, you know, that's a homeboy," he said.

"So if you're a Crip, you're a real nigga?"

"Yeah!" He flashed his gang signal to drive home the point.

"If you're a Blood, you're a real nigga?"

He hesitated for a moment, and one of his homeboys chimed in. "You can be." I glanced at Kevin, and we both nodded, showing that we understood why he had to frame his answer cautiously.

"What am I?" I asked with a smile. Some of the young Crips started to laugh while others smirked with suspicion. *He tryin' to set you up!* "Am I a real nigga?"

They all had something to say about that.

"Nah, man!"

"You a cop!"

"A pig!"

These white guys saw the term solely as a part of their gang subculture and having nothing to do with racial identity. NWA's 1991 album *Niggaz4Life* and songs like "Real Niggaz" and "Real Niggaz Don't Die" had lyrics they identified with, and I came to understand that the term had become a descriptor for those engaged in street life regardless of race and ethnicity. All who aspired to be involved with the gang culture of the

1990s embraced the identity of being "real niggas," and in Salt Lake City that included youth who were Black, white, Latino/Hispanic, Polynesian, Southeast Asian, and even Native Americans from the states that bordered Utah. It was an honorific term among themselves, but I, as a member of law enforcement, was not considered a "real" nigga despite being a Black man.

While the primary objective of the Salt Lake Area Gang Project was to derail the proliferation of gangs and their criminal activity, by means of everything from gathering intelligence to arresting lawbreakers, another part of our mission was diversion—steering young people away from the gang lifestyle. An already difficult task could become impossible if I did not use the tactics that the circumstances required. In our blue jackets, we went to where youth were—parties at skating rinks, picnics in the park, the food court at the mall, and, of course, impromptu gatherings on the street—and conversed with them.

Sometimes those conversations involved giving white gang members a history lesson on the word *nigger* across the street from the Salt Lake Temple. It caused a lot of arguments that were as fun as they were frustrating. But at least we were engaging them.

"I know you think of it as harmless slang, but that word is an element of white supremacy that signified contempt for Black Americans…"

"Aw, come on…"

"Listen, it dismissed any vestiges of our humanity and disregarded our rights to exist on equal footing with whites. When white people use that word, they are communicating to Black people that we are unworthy of white notice, acceptance, or concern."

"You know we don't mean it like *that*."

But I was adamant. "Under no circumstances should a person who is not of our community—especially if they're white—use the term *nigga* as a point of personal reference," I said. "You cannot get away with it."

"If you all can do it, why can't we do it?"

"Because you ain't Black," I said. They couldn't argue with that fact. "You haven't lived our existence." And I meant it.

But I didn't like Black kids using the word either. When I broke down the same history of the term for them, I posed that question as part of the lesson. "So do you believe that whites should be allowed to call us niggas?"

"Nah, man, I'll bust a white man in the mouth if he calls me a nigger."

"But you are calling yourself a nigger," I said, conjuring the same resistance as the white Crips did. "You're calling this brother a nigger. You calling these women over here niggers." That especially annoyed me. "How can you say that?"

And every time they looked at me like I was crazy. "Nigga, get outta here!"

The Black kids were completely ignorant of their own racial history and were proud to be associated with that demeaning term when historically this embrace was not the norm it is today. Folklorist Dr. John Roberts wrote about how much Black people detested the word *nigger* after Emancipation, in part because its popularity among white people increased during

Reconstruction. In other words, the more empowered Black people became, the more white supremacists clung to the epithet. But Dr. Roberts also acknowledged that African Americans not only retained the word but also varied its use among themselves, from using it as a term of endearment to seeing it as a descriptor of behavior that reflected poorly on the community. (An extremely popular example was the "Niggas vs. Black People" set of Chris Rock's 1996 stand-up comedy special "Bring the Pain," which ironically was inspired by the song "Us"—a track on the gangster rapper Ice Cube's 1991 platinum album *Death Certificate*.)

So as strongly as I disagreed with its use, I did understand why young people clung to the N-word. Despite its white supremacist origins, Black people have reimagined the racial epithet into an expression of self-empowerment; this did not start with hip-hop, nor has it been confined to hip-hop. Before Tupac Shakur redefined it as "N-ever I-gnorant G-etting G-oals A-ccomplished," Martin Luther King Jr. played the dozens and used the word among his entourage. In 2008 Jesse Jackson criticized Barack Obama for "telling niggers how to behave." Almost everybody in the Black community says it, and some do as a term of solidarity.

But I never stopped trying to convince them that there was nothing honorable about being called a nigger. "It is not a beautiful word; it's ugly and should not be used at all," I told the Black kids. They often rolled their eyes, but they always heard me out. "And you all are promoting it, degrading yourself and your race."

I felt the same way about the kids' prolific use of the word *bitch*. bell hooks wrote that the sexist language glorified in gangster rap reflected the prevailing values of our "white supremacist capitalistic patriarchy" necessary to uphold "the dominant culture as always an expression of male deviance." The sexuality in early rap music is even more pronounced today, and while the explicitness no longer seems to be the source of aggravation it was in the past, the long-standing and pervasive use of derogatory terms for women still is. The constant referral to "bitches" and "hos" (whores) has never receded. These remain fighting words if you're not a woman using them among her friends.

And given the effects of slavery in the United States, for the social injustices that gave rise to gangster rap to inspire many of these same musical artists to, with impunity, demean women as nothing more than sexual objects that can be purchased via financial success is a tragic irony. Refusing to be victims of white societal emasculation, gangster rappers have reversed the systemic reduction of their manhood to physical labor by eagerly flaunting their sexual prowess. And yet by drawing this symbolic line in the sand with their explicitly misogynistic lyrics, they have overemphasized their masculinity through the psychological subjugation of women.

Because of this understanding, even when I came to appreciate the cultural value of hip-hop, I never approved of its continued misogyny and attempted to share this historical knowledge with the young people on the streets of Salt Lake City. "How can you call any woman but especially a Black woman a bitch?" I would ask the Black boys. "That word has been used over centuries to erase and deny their humanity, and you're promoting it through these lyrics."

I challenged the girls, too, whenever one turned up the volume on Snoop Dogg or Eazy-E and screamed, "That's my jaaaam!"

"How is that your jam?" I said, ignoring her eye rolls and dismissive waves. "He just degraded you. How would you feel if I called you a bitch?"

"Well, I ain't no bitch," she would say with all the neck movements. "Don't be calling me no bitch!"

"Yeah, but if I say it, you don't like it. If this person over here who you don't know says it—especially a white person—you want to get mad. But if this person right here—your boyfriend, this Black gang member, or somebody else in your circle—calls you a bitch, you have no problem with it."

Whatever their race or gender, the young people of Salt Lake City came to know me as Sergeant Stallworth. Sometimes they just called me Stallworth. Or sometimes to the extreme, they would say, "You a crazy motherfucker!"

Now, that I took as a compliment.

Although certain people in Utah would call me a motherfucker because they learned they better not call me nigger.

CHAPTER 11:

SKINHEADS

One night Kevin and I made a routine patrol of the skinhead bar in downtown Salt Lake City. While our task force focused on Crips and Bloods, we monitored the white supremacists too, because they fit the description: a distinct style of dress, hand signals, vandalism to mark their turf...all criteria that qualified them as a gang. Just like Crips and Bloods, the skinheads in Utah also participated in the drug trade and violence, holding stomp parties where they beat people by stomping them with their steel-toed Doc Martens boots. And true to the culture of Mormon Country, many skinheads were born and bred members of the Church of Jesus Christ of Latter-Day Saints.

I walked into the bar expecting these white supremacists to test me for daring to step into their territory. It was my job.

I had to let them know we were watching them, ready and willing to confront any criminal behavior on their part. As with any other gang, my objective was to make the skinheads uncomfortable doing their unlawful business while remaining myself within the confines of the law. In other words, I couldn't punch somebody in the mouth for calling me a fucking Black nigger.

Yet the minute we walked through the door, the skinheads bombarded me with their racist hatred.

"Fuck niggers!"

"Black nigger!"

"Fucking nigger!"

The barrage fired at me continued as Kevin and I continued through the bar. "You okay?" he asked.

"I'm fine," I assured him. "Stay alert. Things are about to take off." After giving me a quizzical look, Kevin smiled. We hadn't been partners for long but he already knew me well enough to know that I wasn't going to let this fly. I had a response for these racists and would resort to a different kind of language they would understand. *Don't fuck with me*, the skinheads were going to learn. *I'm not to be played with.*

One skinhead made his contempt for my Black presence especially obvious, rising to his feet and making hard eye contact with me. Along with his shaved head, he was arrayed in full "uniform"—jeans, Doc Martens steel-toed boots, suspenders, and an olive-green flight jacket adorned with a swastika, Iron Cross, and other Nazi insignia, along with a pin of the Confederate flag. With a smile on my face and in the most professional way, I approached this despicable excuse for a human being. "Can I speak to you for a minute?"

Kevin rolled his eyes as if to say, *Oh, shit!*

"What do you want?" the skinhead replied, practically spitting the words at me.

"You look like a decent-looking guy to me," I said innocently. "I haven't been with a white woman in a while, and I'd like to give my 'assets' to a deserving one. You know what they say. *The blacker the berry, the sweeter the juice.* I think your mother might be the one worthy of my skills."

As murmurs of "fucking nigger" and "Black motherfucker" flew through the bar, I observed Kevin subtly reach under his blue Salt Lake Area Gang Project jacket and place his right hand on the butt of his gun.

I continued my polite harangue of the skinhead who'd participated in the verbal assault on me. "Speaking of motherfucker, I desperately want to fuck yours. I really wish you would introduce me to your mother so I can show her what being with a 'real' man is like instead of inchworm motherfuckers like your father."

Losing all control, the skinhead lunged toward me. "My mother doesn't fuck niggers!" His friend threw his arms around the guy to prevent him from leaping on me.

"You know what they say. *Once you go Black, you never go back,*" I said. "Once you set me up with your mother, she'll swear off sex with punk-ass bitches like you and your dad and give her creamy white body to Black men like me."

"I'll kill you, nigger!" the skinhead kept yelling, nearly

in tears of rage as his friend continued to restrain him. "My mother would never fuck a nigger!"

"I think she already did. Because you look like you have a little Black in you. You know, big lips and nose like a chimpanzee."

The bar patrons expressed their displeasure in angry, hushed tones. Hand still on his gun, Kevin led me toward the exit. As I followed, I made eye contact with as many of these white supremacists as I could. Near the exit, another skinhead invaded my personal space, echoing the first one's threat to kill me. But when I pulled out my 9mm Glock and pressed it to his forehead, the skinhead quickly retreated without another word.

As Kevin and I made our way to our car, the bar full of skinheads congregated by the door, yelling racial epithets at me. I smiled smugly, finding satisfaction in fighting back and defeating them psychologically. I had successfully weaponized against them the same racist beliefs that resulted in the lynching of Black men throughout the history of AmeriKKKa: the piety and purity of white womanhood.

"You really pissed them off," Kevin said, grinning at me. And that was the pragmatic nature of our partnership. Whenever I improvised our interaction with an individual or group, Kevin didn't question my actions. He simply flowed with me in the moment and backed my play. We had quickly developed an unspoken, inherent trust in each other, and that strengthened the bond between us.

A week later Kevin and I paid another visit to the skinhead bar. I was not going to let them think they had intimidated me with their verbal attacks and threats to kill me. When we walked in, there were murmurings of "fucking pigs" but not one declaration of "Black nigger" or "Black motherfucker." Clearly a lesson had been learned.

But much more had to be taught.

CHAPTER 12:

DENIAL IS NOT A LAKE IN UTAH

The late 1980s saw a major influx of members of the Tongan Crip Gang from Inglewood, California, to Salt Lake City. With them came a spike in violence as they traded drive-by shootings and firebombings with their rivals, particularly those living in the predominantly Hispanic neighborhood of Glendale on the west side of the city. That night Kevin and I rushed to the scene of the latest firebombing in time to catch some TCGs running from a burning home. As I cuffed one, I noticed a small book in his back pocket.

As Kevin and I processed them, we emptied their pockets, and several of these young Polynesian men had the same book in their possession. I opened one and flipped through the pages, some of which had notes in the margins and lines highlighted. "Kevin," I said as I held up the book. His face mirrored the shock and confusion I was feeling. While these Tongan Crips were drive-by shooting and firebombing, they were carrying miniature versions of the Book of Mormon in their back pockets.

"So you're a Mormon," I said to the young man I was booking. How could these Mormon Crips identify with both their gang and their church? "If your gang asks you to kill a fellow Mormon on the other side of the color line," I asked, the opposing color being Blood red, "would you do it?"

Unbothered by the disparate actions dictated by these opposing identities, he shrugged and said, "I will attack my enemies if they get in my way."

"Why are you all carrying this while gangbanging?"

He gave me a blank stare as if the answer should have been obvious. "We're studying for our mission."

The Church of Latter-Day Saints strongly encourages its members to do missionary work with the objective of spreading the gospel and expanding its ranks. A typical mission for male Mormons lasts for two years and may even take them to foreign countries. In preparation for their assignments, missionaries attend one of the church's ten training centers, the largest one being in Provo, Utah. There they learn how to teach the gospel and, if they're assigned to a foreign country, the language of its people.

The most important thing to note about missionary work is that the Church of Latter-Day Saints does not require its members to complete this service. Nor does it fund these missions or pay its missionaries. Except for the transportation to their destination, aspiring missionaries finance their own expeditions and volunteer their time. Yet approximately one out of three young Mormon men voluntarily make this commitment to proselytize across the country and even the globe.

And some of them are gang members.

More mind boggling than the ease with which these young people lived out these contradictory allegiances was the resistance I faced when I attempted to enlist Mormon leaders into our anti-gang efforts. The Church of Latter-Day Saints dominates Utah and particularly Salt Lake City. Virtually every aspect of life revolves around the social and religious mores of the Mormon faith, and the introduction of gang culture and gangster rap into the laid-back dynamic of this conservative society proved unsettling. Given the dominance of this religious authority, I presumed the church would be an eager and influential partner with the Salt Lake Area Gang Project in its mission to stop the growth of gangs.

I was wrong. When I and others in the criminal justice field attempted to sound the alarm about the emerging threat from street gangs, the church would not accept that its faith was failing their children. Some influential Mormons in and beyond the church even attributed the threat of gangs to race.

The state senate majority leader was an especially egregious example. "The number of these Mexican kids involved in gangs is inconsequential to Utah society," he once told me in a private conversation. He was a powerful individual in the state legislature, and I'd approached him in the hallway at the Utah State Senate with the expectation that he would be a powerful ally in

securing public funding and enacting policies for anti-gang initiatives. "They should not be allowed to commit drive-by shootings, firebombings, beer thefts from 7-Eleven stores, assaults,
et cetera without having to face the most serious consequences
for their actions, and they deserve to be treated in the harshest
manner that Utah law allows." He even went as far as to say that
the Utah legislature should authorize funds to build a juvenile
detention facility surrounded by a twelve-foot-high electrified
fence in the desert west of the Great Salt Lake. "We wouldn't
need guards. Just turn the current on and let them have at it
with their conflict with one another."

My initial reaction to what I perceived to be the state senator's ill-timed and ignorant attempt at dark humor was a nervous chuckle.

"I'm not joking," he said without a hint of levity on his face
or in his tone of voice. "We cannot afford to let these criminals prey on honest, decent people. Hopefully, they would try
to escape and allow the current to settle the matter for Utah
citizens."

I quickly stopped laughing, unable to allow this alarming,
nightmarish, and coldhearted demand for youth imprisonment
and potential horrifying execution to stand unchallenged.
"Senator, your solution is ill conceived, totally without merit,
and completely absurd," I said. "Confining juveniles with an
electrified fence would be interpreted as a form of cruel and
unusual punishment under the Fourteenth Amendment's right
to due process." My lifelong appreciation for Hispanic culture
also compelled me to call out the senator's racist singling out

of Mexican kids for such inhumane treatment. "What about the white and Polynesian kids who are known to be members of the Mormon Church—*your* church—who are equally guilty of committing the same crimes you so self-righteously attribute solely to Mexicans? You do realize, don't you, that some of our more notorious gang members are Tongan and Samoan Mormons? They too would be subject to your electrified fence form of justice. Your solution reeks of elitist racism."

Rather than respond to that challenge, the senate majority leader gave me a piercing stare and dismissively walked away. We never spoke again.

And that Mormon state senate leader who presumed that the religious upbringing of white Mormon youth rendered them innocent was not an outlier. On the contrary, when they rallied in defense of their faith, the members of the church were prone to implicate race and culture. In Utah, Mormons tend to be either white or Polynesian, and they focused on the racial distinction between the two groups as the source of the gang problem. Despite their shared faith, they viewed the Polynesian youth—the "non-white minority"—differently. Only the white Mormon youth were innocent. *It was racism, pure and simple.* This differentiation occurred even among my Mormon friends who professed to be unbiased in their upbringing and outlook. When I dared to say that Mormon youth were dismissing their biblical upbringing and the teachings of their most revered text, the Book of Mormon, to engage in gang activity, I occasionally found myself accused of being anti-Mormon for telling the truth.

The most jarring reaction among members of the church came from white students. I often gave presentations on the campus of Brigham Young University, the flagship school of the Mormon faith, and they dashed any hopes that I might forge inroads into the Mormon Church through its young congregants. Instead the students challenged me at every presentation.

"The fact is, the church is at the heart of a substantial number of problems with gangs along the Wasatch Front in the north-central part of Utah."

"With all due respect, Sergeant Stallworth, but the gang violence—the drive-bys, the robberies, the assaults—isn't that mostly committed by Blacks, Hispanics, and Polynesians?" one said. Anticipating where his argument was headed, his classmates nodded with approval. "The problem here is culture. *Their* culture," he insisted. "It has nothing to do with the Mormon Church."

"The Polynesian gang members we encounter are almost always Mormons just like you," I said, invalidating that argument. "They are such devout Mormons that at the time of their arrests, they have copies of the Book of Mormon in their possession because they're studying for their missions. They're responding to the highest calling of your faith."

Then I shared the irrefutable statistics I had collected: Not only did the local gangs have Mormon members, they were white as well as Polynesian.

I always hoped that each group of BYU students would be different than the last, but they had the same reaction I had come to expect from the Mormon leaders to whom I offered the same evidence: unmitigated denial.

"White Mormon gang members just *don't* exist."

"Even if those statistics are true…"

"They're not!"

"…they couldn't possibly be *true* Mormons."

"Right! They're not devoted!" I heard that often despite how many white gang members were also preparing for their two-year missions while gangbanging around Salt Lake. Polynesian or white, these young people would proudly declare their faith at the time of their arrests, and when I followed up with their ward bishops, not only would they verify their membership in the church, they also would describe their avid participation. "They're *bastardizing* the faith."

"You're attributing the involvement of Polynesian Mormons in violent street gangs to their cultural shortcomings while also using race to exonerate white Mormons for the same activities," I said. "How does the Mormon Church justify knowing that any of its youth are engaging in this lifestyle yet looking away?"

"The problem, Sergeant Stallworth, is that you're prejudiced against Mormons!"

From the ranks of law enforcement to the seats of governmental power, the Mormon culture permeates everything in Utah, and while I respect the religion of others to a certain point, I neither accept things blindly nor care for religious leaders who ignore my hard-earned expertise. In fact, I welcomed head-butting contests with them. I have a hard head.

My persistence in the face of denial often led to accusations of my being anti-Mormon, and while I would never accuse the community of racially discriminating against me, I still found it unfair for some of its members to accuse me of religious bias for stating facts. The emerging gang problem was a serious threat that warranted a police response. Not just any response but the *right* response, and we the police could not act in ways that threatened the very community we were trying to help.

"That's bullshit," said Kevin. "You're the most non-racist person I know. Some of the biggest racists I've ever encountered have been within my own faith." Because he never brought up race, I took Kevin's validation as an extreme compliment. Himself a devout member of the Mormon Church, Kevin accepted that when it came to gangs, the state authorities of his faith were refusing to exercise leadership on this issue and, as a result, failing Utah's youth.

One devout Mormon youth who took the long road to redemption was a Tongan Crip named Maile "Miles" Kinikini. He was a good kid—when not engaging in gang activity—and Kevin and I had a lot of fun with him. The young man clearly loved his religion, but he was as committed to his gang. In fact, Miles was so committed to both, he raised hell on one of the most important days on the Mormon calendar.

CHAPTER 13:

CHASING MILES

Miles Kinikini was born into the religion and came of age in the gang. Devout Mormons who wanted to be "at the feet of the Prophet," his parents moved their family to Salt Lake City where he was born. They landed in Glendale, a neighborhood on the west side of the city where several Hispanic gangs were already active. While not as numerous or organized, the neighborhood Polynesian kids began to clash with them. When Miles was in the third grade, he was walking home from school with several friends when a group of older Hispanic kids ambushed them on bikes and attacked them with bats and knives.

"I looked up and saw one of the guys get hit on the side of the head with a bat," Miles recalled many years later in an interview with the podcast *All My Friends Are Felons*, hosted by former "prison academy principal" and fellow Utahn Mark Hugentobler. At ten years old, he realized that none of them could safely venture out alone on the streets of Salt Lake City. "I had a couple of relatives that got stabbed in junior high as a result of the tension." And Miles wanted to retaliate. He and his homeboys would harass Hispanic kids they "caught slippin'," even if they were not involved with gangs. "A lot of the enemies that we had we made."

By the time he was in the eighth grade, Miles was the heart of this emerging gang in Salt Lake City when an OG from Los Angeles—a high school sophomore—moved to Glendale. Often Polynesian parents on the West Coast sent their children to live with relatives in Utah in the hope of whisking them away from the influence of gangs, unaware that Mormon Country, too, had fallen prey to them. The young OG gave Miles's crew guidance and structure, and they became officially affiliated with the Tongan Crips Gang.

When I met Miles at the age of fourteen, he was among those Mormon gang members studying for his mission when not firebombing the home of rivals. Most Polynesians grow to be very tall and powerfully built, and at six-two and two hundred pounds, Miles was considered small. He probably could have picked me up and broken me in two, but fortunately, he had the mind of a middle schooler, and that gave me an advantage.

I liked Miles. He had a funny sense of humor with a penchant for telling tall tales in which he was the hero. Even when I was pissed at him and wanted to slap him upside the head, I would chuckle to myself at some of the stuff that came out of his mouth. It made sense that other young people gravitated to Miles and that he rose in the ranks of the TCG. He had a cousin he admired and feared who played for the Philadelphia Eagles. "If you don't straighten out your act," I sometimes told him, "I'm going to call your cousin and get him to come kick your ass." We developed enough of a rapport with Miles that he confessed that his uncle had forbidden him to go on his mission. "Because of my involvement with the gang," he said with a mixture of disappointment and acceptance as he looked down at his Nike sneakers. Still, Miles continued to be active in both the gang and the church.

July 24 is Pioneer Day—a state holiday in Utah commemorating the time when Brigham Young established the Mormon community in Utah by leading an exodus of 147 Mormons from Nauvoo, Illinois, through the Rocky Mountains to the Great Salt Lake Valley after an armed mob assassinated the church's founding president. The church has celebrated this date since 1849, and it's bigger than the Fourth of July. On the night of July 23, 1992, people already were gathering along the two-mile annual Pioneer Day parade route to get the best seats.

The gang unit was patrolling the area on foot when we heard *pop, pop, pop!* Someone was shooting a gun. We ran toward the sound of the gunfire but could not find the culprit amid the chaos on State Street, a sprawling six-lane thoroughfare that becomes unbearably hot in late July. Later we would learn that the shooting was a retaliation in an increasingly violent conflict between two Polynesian gangs that began a few months earlier at a nightclub. A TCG leader was dating the sister of a Samoan Crip, and while the sets were not rivals, they were far from allies. While both gangs were at the club, the Tongan Crip struck the girl, she ran to her brother, and the ensuing altercation between the two gangs spilled out into the parking lot. Several leaders of the TCG got into a truck and ran it into the Samoan gang, killing three of them.

Soon after the incident Kevin and I identified the Pioneer Day shooter as none other than Maile "Miles" Kinikini. Every Pioneer Day the TCG congregated in front of the Federal Building to party. Already wasted from the previous night, eighteen-year-old Miles was among over two hundred Tongan youth when about eight cars filled with Samoan gangbangers rolled up. "We're gonna kill you Tongans!" they yelled before firing at the crowd with 12-gauge shotguns and scattering them across State Street. High on both alcohol and acid, Miles fired back at the Samoans, then ran for two blocks to jump into a friend's car and peel off.

Once Kevin and I identified Miles as the Pioneer Day shooter, we set out to catch him.

We literally chased Miles. Kevin and I would spot him in Rose Park or at the Crossroads (a now extinct mall once owned by the Mormon Church), and when he saw us, he would take off running. Miles may have been large but he was also young, and we couldn't keep up with him. We had attempted to corner him, and because Mormons are very strict about attending weekly sacrament meetings, Kevin and I eventually showed up at Miles's church on Sundays. We only found him there one time, but once again, he spotted us and took off, and we lost him.

This chase went on for a year until one day we finally cornered Miles and brought him in. I sat him down. "Do you realize the opportunities that you have in life?" I asked. "You weren't raised to be a gang member, and your faith is against what you're doing as well. You realize that?"

"Yeah."

"Why you do it?"

"I believe in my Mormon faith. One hundred percent," said Miles. "But I also believe in being a Crip. I'm a Crip and will always be a Crip."

"Mormonism doesn't teach drive-by shootings. Mormonism doesn't teach throwing Molotov cocktails at your enemies' houses. How do you reconcile the two?" He just stared at me. "There're really two places for you, Miles. You're either going to jail for a long period of time, or you're going into a grave," I said. "You need to rethink what you're doing."

Sadly, my warning proved to be prescient. For the Pioneer Day shooting, Miles was convicted of possession of a deadly weapon with intent to kill. He served two years, but it would not be his last bid.

Many years later, in the mid-2000s, I would attend the annual gang conference in Salt Lake City and see the name Maile Kinikini on the program. I took a seat in the front row at the session where he was a guest speaker, and when they introduced him, we caught each other's eye. "I want to introduce you to somebody," Miles told the audience before asking me to stand up. "This is Sergeant Stallworth. This son of a bitch and his partner chased me for a year and caught me. Sergeant Stallworth was the only one who ever tried to get me out of the game."

Miles paused to address me. "You remember that, Sergeant? You're the only one who told me that if I didn't do right and get straight, I was gonna end up dead or in prison. Well, you were halfway right." While serving his sentence for the Pioneer Day shooting, Miles recommitted to Mormonism and his family. In fact, after his release, he completed his mission in Northen California, returned to Salt Lake City, and began a family.

But gang ties—and impulses—die hard. Miles had a younger cousin who had joined the Tongan Crips, and their rivalry with the Baby Regulators landed Miles in prison after they committed a drive-by shooting at his aunt's house in Glendale. The rival gang fired on a parked car in front of her home and barely missed her one-year-old grandchild sitting inside the vehicle. Intent on retaliation, Miles and several of his cousins drove to the homes of two adversaries they suspected had committed the drive-by, threw two gallons of gasoline on their homes, and set them on fire. Caught and convicted, Miles spent another year in jail for second-degree arson.

Even though Miles had ignored my foresight, he never forgot and appreciated my effort to set him on the right path at an early age. He explained to the audience that he had gone to prison for a few years, but the experience taught him to get out and do right. In front of everyone, Miles thanked me for attempting to help him. At the time of that conference, he was married with four children and another on the way, and the big kid had become a big man—over two hundred pounds. When I approached him after the session ended, Miles wrapped his arms around me and picked me up off the carpet like a baby.

After he put me down, Miles told me he was a used car salesman and tried to get me to drop by his dealership. "Man, I'm not going to give you all my private information!" I said.

"But I'm not doing 'that' anymore," he said.

"I don't care. I ain't giving you all my private information."

So while Maile Kinikini failed to sell me a used car, I do consider him a success story.

Miles was an exception to the norm. For too many young Mormons, the allegiance to gangs was beating out the devotion to their faith. I told the adults in their lives that the involvement of Mormon youth in gangs was not a negative reflection on their religion, but they had to figure out why they were turning to gangs for a sense of community and belonging. Except for Kevin, they insisted that their faith was infallible. It took everything I had not to say, *Your faith is crap and failing these kids.* No one was willing to see past their religion and accept the fact that when not attending sacrament meetings, these children were throwing Molotov cocktails through windows in West Salt Lake City.

CHAPTER 14:

ONETIME PASS

Every hardened gang member was once a kid having his first run-in with the law. Often the transgression was something minor like vandalism, shoplifting, or the possession of cigarettes or alcohol. Recognizing that he was a gang member or potentially affiliated with one, the officers on the scene might come down hard on him. Although the kid had no record and the infraction was minor, they cuffed him, tossed him in the back of the squad car, booked him at the station, and made him sit in a jail cell until an exasperated parent or guardian could be contacted and pulled from a day's work to take custody of him.

Kevin and I took a different approach when faced with this scenario. Upon realizing that the kid had never been in any trouble before we encountered him, instead of transporting him to juvenile detention, we gave him a ride home. Several years after moving to Utah, Micki and I had another son. Now the father of two boys, I wanted to extend to these parents the courtesy I would want to receive if either Brandon or Nico was flirting with trouble.

"Are you Freddy's mother?"

"Yes. What happened?"

"He was caught trying to steal a bottle of Old English at the store."

"Freddy what?"

"And when we asked him why he stole the beer, he admitted that he did it as a favor to an older boy he met in the park. We checked into him, and the boy who sent Freddy to get the beer is a known member of the Crips. You do understand who the Crips are."

"Oh my God yes, they're that gang!"

"Yes, ma'am. It appears that your son shoplifted the beer to impress this Crip. We understand that this is alarming, and that it can be very difficult as a working parent to keep tabs on your child. I have two boys myself. But I strongly encourage you to play a more active role in keeping Freddy out of the gangs' clutches."

"Thank you."

"Understand that this is a onetime courtesy."

"I understand. Thanks again, Sergeant Stallworth."

The astonished look on these parents' faces always gave way to expressions of gratitude. As they told Kevin and me on multiple occasions, they had never heard of cops giving an offender—their child—a break when we rightfully could place them into police custody.

Our onetime-pass approach proved fruitful, allowing us to establish a bond and gradually build trust among members of the minority community who saw firsthand that we were "unconventional" cops.

Intelligence, suppression, and diversion: These were the pillars of the Salt Lake Area Gang Project from its start. Much law enforcement efforts to address gang-related issues focused on the first two: gathering information on members and stopping their criminal activities. But when I designed the gang unit, I always intended for diversion—steering young people away from the gangs—to be just as important. My position has always been that youth who become involved in gangs always get out; the question is how. We had to do whatever was in our power to encourage them to leave gangs—if not avoid them altogether—before prison or death were the only exits that remained. From a law enforcement perspective that included building relationships with the adults who held sway in their lives, and as much as possible diverting individuals from the criminal justice system into alternative programs that hopefully could put their lives on a positive path. The only Black legislator in the state house of representatives, Duane Bordeaux, had a program called Colors of Success that worked with gang youth, monitoring and mentoring them, helping them finish their education and secure jobs. Duane was a Utah native and a graduate of the University of Utah and very good at what he did for the kids. The scope of law enforcement's ability to divert young people from the lure of gangs is narrowly defined. This is why we must work with parents, educators, elected officials, and other community leaders, each of us playing our specific role to set youth on the path to positive lifestyles. Easier said than done.

The belief that police are not to be trusted is commonplace, long-standing, and, sadly, historically valid. Minority parents especially harbored distrust toward the gang unit. Other Black parents considered me untrustworthy because I was a cop. White Mormon parents occasionally accused me of being anti-Mormon while Polynesian parents—the vast majority of whom were Mormon—charged me with being antagonistic toward both the Mormon Church *and* Polynesian culture. Hispanic-Latino parents assumed Kevin and I were biased against their children because they were not white, and Asian parents called us "anti–yellow man." The penchant of some community activists and media outlets to sensationalize gang issues toward their own agenda made our efforts to build rapport with minority communities and divert vulnerable youth from gangs even more difficult.

Because law enforcement has not always been fair and honest in its dealings with racial and other minorities, cops must earn the trust of these communities, and this takes time. Given how quickly gangs were on the rise, time was a luxury we never had. We lost even more because of our colleagues' initial denial that gangs were even present in Utah, never mind a serious threat.

When elected officials and law enforcement leaders finally accepted that gangs had infiltrated the community and felt pressured to respond to the spike in crime, they made decisions that either ignored or undermined the strategies that the Salt Lake Area Gang Project proposed as effective responses.

The mayor of Salt Lake City did exactly that when she hired as the chief of police Ruben Ortega, who in turn insisted on employing SWAT officers to address gangs. From its inception, I knew that our unit's approach had to include diversion, but such a proactive and affirmative philosophy is antithetical to the DNA of officers who are trained in special weapons and tactics. They are an aggressive, take-no-prisoners, kick-ass-and-take-names breed of law enforcement. SWAT does not believe in diverting kids from gangs into alternative programs for rehabilitation; they arrest you and that's all.

I expected SWAT leader Sergeant Clark Myers to possess that same DNA, but again I could not allow cynicism to prevent me from attempting to get him on board with Salt Lake Area Gang Project's philosophy and approach. I recognized that we shared an objective with SWAT: to keep the streets of Salt Lake City safe. But in pursuit of that objective, we also gained positive benefits from emphasizing diversion, and I had a faint hope that I could persuade Myers to consider the merits of our approach. Undermining gang activity required more than derailing their criminal activities by taking kids off the street. It also meant steering them toward a proper lifestyle and connecting them to programs and services that could facilitate that. Not every young person needed to be thrown in jail and have a record that followed him for the rest of his life.

But SWAT's position was *Fuck that!*

As Myers listened to my speech, he rolled his eyes, adamant

that he was going to lock up every gang member that he encountered regardless of the degree of the offense. He took their activities as a personal affront. *They're gang members, they crossed me*, Myers thought, *and I'm arresting every one of them.* His destructive approach undermined the cohesiveness of the gang unit as the community increasingly associated Kevin and me with SWAT's aggressive tactics. The more they raided locations and rounded up everyone who was present with no regard to their actual culpability, the more the minority communities resisted our genuine efforts to build positive relationships with them. Painting all gang cops with a broad stroke, they questioned the sincerity of our diversion attempts.

And then there were the parents who were a part of the problem.

"Stallworth, I need you to come into the department." Kevin and I were on patrol in the community when the Salt Lake City chief of police summoned me to his office. As we drove back to the Public Safety Building, I tried to predict what this could be about but nothing came to mind.

When I entered the chief's office, a Hispanic woman was seated across his desk. The chief introduced her as the mother of a young man Kevin and I had encountered on the street a few days earlier. "You labeled my son as a gang member and put him into the database," the woman said. Then she turned back to the chief. "I want to file a complaint against him."

I remembered her son. I had asked him a few questions— routine police intelligence—and his answers hit all the marks. The clothes he had on, the people he associated with, the places they frequented—all the indicators of gang membership. The young man must have told his mother about our conversation because she immediately reported me to the chief.

I appreciated that the chief gave me the opportunity to challenge my accuser, and knowing I had the truth on my side, I proceeded to spell out how her son fit all the criteria that warranted being added to the database. But the way the woman kept disputing my account of what transpired between her son and me even though she wasn't there told me she already knew. "My son is not a gang member!" she interrupted at every turn.

Soon the chief also had enough of her belligerence. "Based on what I've heard, I'm satisfied that the conversation Sergeant Stallworth had with your son, and the conclusion he drew from it, are within the department's protocols," he said. "There is no merit to your complaint."

The woman jumped up in disgust. "And what's the big deal if my son's in a gang?" she yelled. "*I* was a gang member, and it didn't hurt me."

I gave the chief a look. *May I go?*

Yes, you may.

The gangster lifestyle had so permeated the mindset of the young Hispanic-Latino males in Utah that many claimed that being in a gang was part of their cultural heritage. As if society was not already hell-bent on controlling and destroying them, these misguided young men proudly declared their gang ties with the same aplomb they might have proclaimed affiliation with a major college or university. As someone who grew up in El Paso, which is dominated by Mexican culture, this angered me. It infuriated me even more when some of the adults in the lives of these impressionable youth such as this mother reinforced these stereotypes, aiding in the marginalization of their own children. When the head of a family has such a cavalier attitude toward gang involvement, we have little to no chance of diverting her children from that lifestyle. Such parents especially unsettled Kevin, who took the job of working with Hispanic families to redirect their children into more positive activities very seriously.

Even with parents who appreciated our help, we often had to walk a tightrope between our responsibilities as law enforcement and our respect for cultural norms. Just as quickly as I realized how many gang members revere gang affiliations with the same ease they did their religious beliefs, I discovered that the toughest Polynesian gang member upheld the utmost respect and fear for their parents. Kevin and I learned that the hard way.

We had picked up a Tongan kid for some minor infraction, and as we often did, we opted to take him home and turn him over to his parents rather than put him into the system. This kid was as big as Miles, who at six-two and over two hundred pounds was considered small in the Polynesian community. Kevin and I walked him to the front door and rang the bell. His father—who was much bigger than his son—answered the door.

"Sir, we caught your son vandalizing a storefront on South Main Street," I said. "And it's important that you're aware that the graffiti he was tagging is associated with the Tongan Crip Gang."

The father glared at his son as he cowered against the doorway, and Kevin and I continued with our routine conversation. We told him that we preferred not to take his son into custody since he had no prior issues with the law and the offense was minor, but it was imperative that he pay him more attention because he was at high risk of getting embroiled with gangs and worse criminal activity. "We brought him home today, but this is as a onetime courtesy," I said. "We don't want to have to arrest him for something more serious in the future."

As usual in these interactions, the boy's father thanked us for cutting his son slack and bringing him home. Kevin and I bid them both a good evening, but we had barely turned to walk away when we heard it. *Crack!* And seconds later, *THUD!*

Kevin and I turned to look in the direction of the sound. The boy was on the ground, slumped against the doorframe, his father towering over him with his hand balled into a fist. Polynesian parents generally believed in corporal punishment, and he had punched his son as hard as he could in the head.

Kevin and I looked at each other. Because we had witnessed it, we had no choice. I reached for my handcuffs and advanced on the father as Kevin helped the young man to his feet. "You're under arrest for assault."

"What?"

"You have the right to remain silent." I continued to Mirandize the boy's father as I handcuffed him and led him to our car.

As we drove him to the jail, he fumed with confusion in the backseat. "You asked me to get more involved with my children," he said. "I disciplined him, and you arrest me?"

Word of the incident spread in the Polynesian community, and it became a big deal for the department. This was not the first culture clash law enforcement had with them. The police frequently had to shut down backyard luaus, and the Polynesian families could not understand why digging a hole in the ground, filling it up with heated rocks, and slow-roasting a pig was against Salt Lake City ordinances. Days later Kevin and I found ourselves at a community town hall meeting explaining our decision to arrest the man for striking his son. "You cannot hit your children," I said. "It's against the law. If we see you hitting your kids, we must arrest you for assault."

"But this is our culture."

"You have your culture, we have our laws, and our laws supersede your culture."

From that day forward, whenever Kevin and I implemented a onetime pass, once we turned the child over to his parent, we immediately walked away. We could still hear the corporal punishment taking place behind us. But as long as we didn't see it, we had no one to arrest.

CHAPTER 15:

COP KILLER

Sergeant Stallworth, we have some concerns about Mr. T's appearance at our venue," the woman said. She booked acts for the Salt Lake City Fairgrounds, and in forty-eight hours, rapper Ice-T and his heavy-metal band Body Count were scheduled to perform. The Combined Law Enforcement Associations of Texas (CLEAT) had just called for a boycott in response to the group's song "Cop Killer." "We were told to contact you for guidance."

Requests for guidance like this were on the rise—a big difference from my early days in Utah when my insights were undervalued if not outright disregarded. From the moment I listened closely to "Fuck tha Police," I continued to feed my obsession with gangsta rap, and my independent study paid off with deep insight into the inner workings of gangs. The lyrics revealed almost everything you could want to know about the "g-code." I broadened my research into ethnic studies, sociology, history—any discipline that provided the necessary context to better understand gangs. Eager to share my findings with my law enforcement colleagues, I began delivering presentations where I spat lyrics that had ingrained themselves into my psyche and correlated them to aspects of the lifestyle, thereby gaining a nationwide reputation as an expert in gangsta rap and street gangs.

When I worked from home preparing for lectures by studying gangsta rap videos or watching footage of gang activity sent to me by fellow law enforcement from around the country, my older son, Brandon, often sat beside me on the floor under my arm. He watched the videos with me, and I would explain what was going on. "That's a bad word," I would say. "You don't ever say that." Sometimes Brandon had questions, and I did my best to answer them in a way he could understand. As I was studying, he was getting an education of his own. I impressed upon him the importance of doing the right thing. "You never follow anybody, you lead them," I would say. "Stallworth boys are leaders."

As an emerging authority on gangsta rap and street gangs, I was traveling the country to share the knowledge I had cultivated from both thorough research and front-line experience. The ATF was the first federal law enforcement agency in the country to properly address the gang problem and invited me regularly to participate in its training programs. Whenever it held a conference, I was one of the first instructors to present because my lectures were so unique. Rather than play the music and then discuss the lyrics, I rapped the lyrics myself so that the heavy bass line could not interfere with the agents' ability to digest the subject matter. Many people questioned whether I could rap, and in the course of a lecture, I would perform an average of five songs. Nor did I ever give the same lecture twice—the presentation I gave to the afternoon class was always different from the one I delivered in the morning.

Invitations from the DEA and the FBI soon followed. The DEA was forming drug force commands around the country and wanted their agents to understand the day-to-day life of a gang member. To teach at the FBI Academy means that your career has reached a pinnacle because they are very selective about who they invite to speak with their agents.

"I did not learn this stuff in order to talk to you all. What I'm giving you is what's infused in my mind after listening to the music over time and digesting what these rappers are saying," I stressed to my trainees. "Now, if this can happen to a forty-year-old cop who's not versed in hip-hop culture and just occasionally listening to it, imagine what's going on in the minds of the children who are walking around with a boombox or headphones, *deliberately listening to this all the time?*"

Because of my writings and lectures, the former president of the California Gang Investigators Association called me the "foremost law enforcement authority" on gangster rap and its correlation to street gang culture, bestowing on Utah the bona fides rarely achieved by cities and states that are not known to be gang havens. The law enforcement community around the country was fascinated by the incongruous nature of street gangs amid Mormon culture. Like oil and water, the two were not supposed to mix, but as I told my audiences, Utah had the same issues with gangs as Los Angeles. The only difference was scale.

My expanding reputation as a "hip-hop cop" coincided with the height of the culture war against popular music, particularly gangsta rap. The more I learned and lectured, the more I defended the artists' freedom of expression. I have always been a proponent of the First Amendment, but my position—both as a police officer and as a Black man—had its roots in a deeper understanding of the stakes. To divert youth from the gangs and violence, we had to understand their grievances, and their issues were laid bare in the music they were creating and listening to. We had to heed it, not censor it.

So between 1992 and 1997, I found myself engaged in the national debate over the violent, graphic, and explicit lyrics as demands to rein in gangsta rap music were building among both Black and white conservatives in America. Tipper Gore, the wife of then vice president Al Gore, led the social movement to raise awareness of profane lyrics in pop music, particularly rap. After finding her eleven-year-old daughter listening to Prince's "Darling Nikki"—a song that explicitly references masturbation—Tipper had co-founded the Parents Music Resource Center (PMRC) in 1985. The organization consisted of four members—all white women who were the wives of prominent politicians. As their leader, Tipper Gore appeared at several congressional hearings to promote their agenda, and the

result is now recognized as a part of music history: the PAREN-
TAL ADVISORY WARNING sticker that record labels put on the
cover of albums that had graphic images or contained profane
or violent lyrics. Artists considered this censorship, and I viewed
PMRC as a movement of racist and entitled white women.

The most notable Black woman in the censorship crusade
of the time was C. Delores Tucker. A prominent Pennsylvania
politician and longtime civil rights activist who marched with
Dr. Martin Luther King from Selma to Montgomery in 1965,
Ms. Tucker dedicated the last years of her life to condemning sexually profane lyrics in rap music. Contending that the
misogynistic nature of those lyrics threatened the moral foundation of the Black community, she had prominent feminists
like Gloria Steinem and entertainers such as Melba Moore and
Dionne Warwick in her corner. Ms. Tucker and her legion of
followers who were mostly women picketed stores that sold rap
music like Tower Records and Sam Goody and attempted to
convince potential customers not to buy it. On several occasions, her strident demonstrations even resulted in her arrest.
Ms. Tucker also purchased stock in Sony, Time Warner, and
similar companies so she could attend shareholder meetings
and protest their involvement in the production and distribution of rap music.

In fact, her crusade against the genre and all those associated with its creation and proliferation resulted in multiple
lawsuits in which she was either plaintiff or defendant, usually
the former. In 1994 Mrs. Tucker criticized the NAACP for
nominating the late Tupac Shakur for an Image Award for his

performance in the film *Poetic Justice* shortly after his arrest for sexually assaulting a fan in a hotel room. Ms. Tucker and her husband, William, later sued Tupac's estate and five other companies for $10 million, alleging that his "sexually explicit messages, offensively coarse language and lewd and indecent words" about her in the songs "Wonda Why They Call U Bitch" and "How Do U Want It" led to death threats, caused her "emotional distress, slander and invasion of privacy," and inflicted on her husband "a loss of advice, companionship and consortium." (To which Shakur's attorney responded, "I can't wait to hear the testimony on that subject.") These are only a few of the actions C. Delores Tucker took in her mission to accomplish the impossible: the elimination of gangsta rap.

However, the next target of the censorship crusade would face a much more difficult challenge. In the summer of 1991, Ice-T released the song "Cop Killer" in which he called for his homeys to wage war against the police. Over time he offered contradictory interpretations of the song. Ice-T once explained that the character behind the first-person lyrics was a psychopath—an angry Black man who had had enough of heavy-handed police tactics—and that while the song represented the rage of minority communities over the violation of their constitutional rights by rogue cops, it did not advocate for the murder of police officers.

Yet several times in interviews and at concerts, Ice-T did advocate violence against police, including murder. For example, he told the *New Musical Express* in August 1992, "I'd like to take one of them [police] right out in the middle of Lankershim

Blvd. and shoot him in the motherfucking head." During the
LA Rebellion that same year, the rapper was captured on video
saying, "I personally would like to blow some fucking police
stations up…If it was up to me I'd burn the White House down
'cause I'm an anarchist. I'm ready to do this shit."

Recorded by Ice-T with his heavy-metal band Body Count,
"Cop Killer" made few waves until June 1992 when it caught
the attention of the Combined Law Enforcement Associations
of Texas. CLEAT demanded that Time Warner stop distributing the song, and their call spread across the country like a California wildfire. At the peak of the furor, at least five fraternal
law enforcement organizations and support groups representing
approximately five hundred thousand members joined CLEAT's
boycott. The city councils of Houston and Los Angeles adopted
resolutions condemning "Cop Killer." Both President George
H. W. Bush and Vice President Dan Quayle also denounced
the song. Even former national security aide and central figure
in the Iran-Contra affair Oliver North called upon the fifty US
governors to bring criminal proceedings against Time Warner
for "violation of sedition and anti-anarchy statutes."

I entered the fray by contacting Ron DeLord, president of
CLEAT. "Are you sure you want to follow through on this boycott?" I asked. He explained that "Cop Killer" was so offensive to
his membership, the organization felt no choice but to boycott
Ice-T. I felt compelled to make DeLord understand the overall
dynamics of the action he was advocating and the likely result.

Gangster rap lyrics are an intellectual agitation to the body
politic, especially the police establishment. Reflecting the life

experiences of the artists including their issues with police brutality, the lyrics are a deliberate assault on the senses of those
unfamiliar with the ways of hip-hop culture. Furthermore, rappers are very entrepreneurial in nature, doing what they think
is necessary to increase sales of their music, including eagerly
seeking publicity. And if the publicity is negative, *even better for
record sales.*

"In all likelihood, your boycott is going to have the same
result as when the FBI wrote NWA in 1989 to criticize 'Fuck tha
Police,'" I said. The members of NWA gave interviews where
they promoted the fact that the group had garnered the scrutiny of arguably the most powerful and respected law enforcement institution in America. They used the FBI's criticism of
the group to fuel controversy that, in turn, became an effective
marketing tool. "The controversy gave NWA a national pro-
file and made 'Fuck Tha Police' into a youth national anthem
especially for inner-city minorities." Although DeLord understood the law enforcement rationale against boycotting the
song, he insisted that advocating for the killing of cops was
much too volatile for the Texas law enforcement community
not to respond.

"And as a career law enforcement officer, I understand
the passion behind your call for a boycott," I said. "But given
the First Amendment issue and the racial implications here, I
cannot join or in any way support the boycott." I believed that
ensuing clashes between law enforcement and the rap community would generate negative publicity that Ice-T would weap-
onize to increase his music sales and grow his bank account. I

asked DeLord if CLEAT would respond similarly if the controversy involved a country artist, but he ignored my question and
immediately pivoted back to Ice-T. I informed him that I would
be on the opposing side of this debate and wished him well. We
never spoke again.

Other Black members of law enforcement opposed
CLEAT's call to boycott Ice-T. The National Black Police
Association—a fraternal organization of thirty-five thousand
members nationwide—also took a stand for Ice-T's freedom of
speech. "The single 'Cop Killer' is not a call for murder. It is
a form of protest. Ice-T is rapping about police misconduct, a
problem that affects many Americans, primarily poor African
Americans and Latinos," said Ronald E. Hampton, the organization's director for national affairs, in a statement issued
on July 18, 1992. "I am astonished by the level of hypocrisy
expressed by some police organizations, gun owners' groups,
ministers and politicians who have joined the boycott...I did
not see these vocal individuals or organizations showing the
same level of outrage when Rodney King was beaten by four
Los Angeles police officers. Nor did I see the same outrage
when a Simi Valley jury allowed the same four Los Angeles
police officers back on the street."

"What exactly are you concerned about?" I asked the
booker from the Salt Lake City Fairgrounds, smiling at her reference to Ice as Mr. T in that reliable Utahn politeness.

"It is our understanding that Mr. T is a gang member and
could possibly incite gang violence during his performance,
which may result in gun violence."

"Ice-T claims Crip gang affiliation, and I guarantee virtually every Crip in the area will be in attendance. However, his music appeals to all gang members, so that culture will be out in force to listen to a live performance of his music," I explained calmly. "Will he incite violence? Not directly, but you can't predict what his audience will do in response to something he says or others may say. Gangs are unpredictable in that regard." I felt obligated to tell her the truth without understatement or embellishment.

After informing me of the clause in the contract that allowed her to cancel events at the venue, the booker politely ended our conversation. Clearly, she did not care for my advice because Ice-T's event was indeed canceled. Instead of filling the seven-thousand-seat fairgrounds, he was forced to perform at a local Salt Lake City nightclub called DV8. It accommodated approximately one thousand people, so he gave two shows.

Anticipating possible conflicts among rival gangs, the gang unit was present at both, and Kevin and I stood on the balcony to watch the show. Ice-T, who would go on to garner a fortune playing a New York City detective for over two decades on the long-running TV series *Law & Order: Special Victims Unit*, announced our presence to the crowd by pointing toward the balcony while holding a US flag. "This is what I think of this motherfucking shit piece of rag," he yelled as he flossed his butt with the flag. I just laughed at his antics. Then Ice-T extended his middle fingers toward me. Continuing to laugh at him, I returned the gesture.

*   *   *

Prior to the 1993 statewide gang summit, Commissioner of Public Safety Doug Bodrero created and assigned me to the position of the state's gang intelligence coordinator.

The all-encompassing role carried multiple responsibilities: collecting and disseminating data on gangs as well as writing periodic reports on their impact; participating in the suppression of gang activity; training criminal justice personnel and raising community awareness; maintaining relationships with community leaders focused on addressing the gang problem; educating and enlisting the support of legislators; and liaising with the media as partners in the anti-gang response. The commissioner's creation of this position was an acknowledgment of my hard work and accomplishments despite the adversity I encountered on multiple fronts, including from those who should have been natural allies. And whenever controversy surrounded me, Bodrero always backed me. To this day, I am the only person to have held the position of gang intelligence coordinator.

Probably had something to do with all the hell I raised.

CHAPTER 16:

LETTER FROM AN OG

Dear Mr. Stallworth,

I seen you on TV Sunday, the 11th, some of the things you said were true, but let me tell you, all of you, that is Utah are lost when it comes to gangs. I my self have been a Crip an OG for the past 15 years. I know what I'm talking about. I'm with the Rolling 60s. You need to know were the hoods are that will help you. You also need to know who the OGs are that will help you. You need to know were are the sets that will help you. You need alot of help. What you need to do Mr. Stallworth is get to know the OGs that will help you know that next moves. Utah is about money when it comes to us Crips. We look for young kids to do our work, to make the sound for us. There are Bloods out there to, not that many but they are out there. It should help you to know, there are some Crips, some people that want all this over with. But there are some from the hood *that want to keep Utah off they feet so they can come in, "crack$"*

This ain't LA but still the same LA is hear--look and you will find--Q-VO ain't noting but small stuff. Stop it before it gets to big. You can if you look--look for the OGs that ain't hard--we got a way to show who are the OGs. Just look. Mr. Stallworth I like what you have done so far, keep the good work up. Come and see me if you like--but <u>Never</u> let any one read this letter.

CHAPTER 17:

"GANGSTER RAP MADE ME DO IT"

On the evening of April 11, 1992, eighteen-year-old Ronald Ray Howard was driving a GMC Jimmy on a stretch of US Highway 95 near Edna, Texas, while listening to Tupac Shakur's debut album 2*Pacalypse Now* at max volume. With the gunshots and sirens on the track "Soulja's Story" blaring through car speakers, the self-proclaimed member of the Five-Deuce (5-2) Hoover Crips was en route to Houston after a stay in a Gulf Coast town where he had been selling crack cocaine. Then Texas state trooper Bill Davidson appeared behind Howard's vehicle and signaled for him to pull over.

Through his side-view mirror, Howard watched the trooper approach the SUV, his heart pounding hard. On probation for auto theft, he had stolen the SUV. Howard reached for a 9mm handgun loaded with hollow-point bullets and jacked one in the chamber. As Trooper Davidson neared Howard's window, he said, "How are you doing?"

But Howard was already in motion. Bam! With Trooper Davidson only a foot away from him, he fired into his neck and peeled off, Tupac still rhyming in his ears.

But eight people witnessed the shooting, and the seriously injured trooper himself managed to report that he had been shot by a lone Black male. Several hours after the shooting, police apprehended Howard after he crashed the stolen vehicle into a house and attempted to flee on foot. The investigators found the weapon in his possession and also took into evidence the bootleg copy of *2Pacalypse Now* they discovered in the cassette deck of the vehicle. The album contained several songs with graphic depictions of violent confrontations between Black men and people in authority, including the killing of cops.

After listening to the tape, a Texas state trooper interrogating Howard asked him, "Is this why you killed that trooper? Based on what these songs are saying?"

"Yes!"

Three days later the forty-three-year-old father of two would die surrounded by his family, and not only would Ronald Ray Howard face the death penalty for his murder, but gangsta rap also would be placed on trial. "When I think back on it, I used to rap along with tapes about killing cops and talk shit all the time how I'd do it someday," he would say in an interview two weeks after his arrest. "But, damn, there it was. The gun. The music. The cop. It was like the moment of truth. All the hatred came out at once."

When Ronald Ray Howard's capital murder trial began on June 3, 1993, his attorney Allen Tanner would concede the indisputable: Howard killed Trooper Davidson. But at the time of the fatal shooting, he had been listening to Tupac Shakur's "Soulja's Story"—a song that depicts a traffic stop that ends in gunshots.

> *Cops on my tail, so I bail til I dodge 'em*
> *They finally pull me over and I laugh*
> *"Remember Rodney King?" and I blast on his punk ass*
> *Now I got a murder case*

Howard believed Davidson pulled him over for no reason, and gangster rappers say that when cops mess with you for no reason, you've got to fight back. You have to kill them. Howard deserved to be punished, Tanner said, but because of the influence of gangsta rap, he should face life in prison and not lethal injection.

And as part of Howard's "gangster rap made me do it" defense, Tanner asked me to testify as an expert witness.

I made it clear to Tanner that as a career peace officer, I could not support any individual accused of killing a fellow cop; nor did I agree that the music incited Howard to kill Trooper Davidson. If Tanner still wanted me to take the stand, he had to agree to certain conditions. "I can only define the music he was listening to and draw a correlation to the lifestyle he was leading."

Tanner could ask me questions regarding Ronald Ray Howard himself with one exception. While I was on the stand, he could not ask me if I thought his client deserved the death penalty. "I can't do that," I warned Tanner. Howard had killed a fellow member of law enforcement, and I would support the court's ruling on his punishment even if it sentenced Howard to death. "Be very careful of what you ask me."

Tanner agreed to my terms, and in a subsequent meeting with all the attorneys involved in the case—prosecution, defense, and civil litigators—I requested all the information they had gathered on Howard's upbringing. As an intelligence officer, I needed to know everything I could—his family and friends, likes and dislikes, ambitions and obstacles. Understanding that each side had compiled information on Howard to make their respective case arguments, I wanted to make my own interpretations as I prepared my testimony.

The eldest of three children, Howard had been raised in the South Park section of Houston, Texas, by his grandmother and mother who was still in her teens when she gave birth to him. Unfortunately, his father fit the stereotypical image of the absentee father. When he was present, he severely abused Howard starting at the age of three, beating him with a belt and then later using two extension cords braided together. On one occasion, the wounds from his father's beating were so severe that they left streaks of blood when Howard rubbed against the wall behind him. Howard's father also introduced him to marijuana at the age of two by "blowing him a charge" (blowing marijuana smoke in his face) to induce sleep when the boy was too active.

As numerous studies have cited, the absence of a boy's father increases the likelihood of his growing up in poverty, doing poorly in school, having low self-esteem, engaging in sexual activity at an early age, and participating in delinquent behavior, and Howard went down that destructive path. At the age of fourteen, he fathered his first child and would go on to have six children by four different women. One of Howard's children would be born while he was in jail awaiting trial for the murder of Trooper Davidson.

When Howard dropped out of school in the eighth grade, he was unable to read beyond second-grade level. (And his mother would charge the school system with failing him by not giving him the attention needed to overcome his learning deficiency.) To further his education, Howard enrolled in the Job Corps, where he became exposed to the 5-2 Hoover Crips, an LA-based gang whose members had ties to Houston and Louisiana. His stint in Job Corps did not last due to frequent disciplinary actions.

After leaving the program, Howard began selling drugs even as he moved from one minimum-wage job to another. Like too many young people growing up in toxic environments, he felt cheated by the low wages of fast-food restaurants. Rather than continue his education and rise up the professional ladder, Howard sought the immediate acquisition of money and power available through illegal activities. Selling drugs elevated

Howard's social status among his friends, and he spoke of how he would "show off and do all kinds of crazy things" while playing the street game.

At the age of sixteen, he had his first encounter with the criminal justice system when he was arrested for auto theft. At the time Trooper Davidson pulled him over in the stolen truck because of a broken headlight, Howard estimated that he had stolen over three hundred cars. Ironically, he once was shot by the owner of a vehicle he had stolen.

Based on my understanding of Howard's background, the elements of hip-hop culture, and the Black community in general, I felt prepared to testify yet also found my position in this case as an expert witness highly complicated and ironic. When I testified before Congress, my objective was straightforward: to share my knowledge of gangs and the corresponding significance of gangster rap music. And when I spoke with local politicians, law enforcement leadership, and Mormon Church officials about gang activity in the state of Utah, I delivered unvarnished truth even as my insights were unwelcomed. In these circumstances I never softened disturbing facts to please anyone.

But my testimony in Ronald Ray Howard's capital murder trial—and later in the civil lawsuit that Trooper Davidson's widow would file against Tupac Shakur and his music label Time Warner—demanded nuance. My statements required a balanced discussion of racial injustice, respect for the police, and constitutional rights. I had to explain why gangster rap was a valid sociological expression for inner-city minority youth, yet I also felt an obligation to denounce the idea that the music could be legitimately used as a defense for killing a police officer.

When I took the stand in Howard's capital murder trial, I made several key points. First, I explained that gangster rappers became role models for the hip-hop nation in the 1990s because they arose from the same socioeconomic conditions as their core audience. Recording artists and their ardent fans alike viewed the police as the enforcers of the white political power structure in the United States that denied them educational, social, and cultural opportunities—the "occupying army" who buttressed a corrupt system intent on subjugating inner-city minority youth. For these youth—and youth culture in general, but especially those involved with gangs—projecting an image of toughness such as saying "crazy stuff" and flaunting certain attributes are common behavioral traits. These traits create an endless cycle in which achieving status hinges on cultivating a firmly established reputation among one's peer group and frequently centers on assertions of manhood as defined by gang members: sexual conquests, courage, and the mental toughness to succeed in the hustling life of the streets. As part of this expression, gangster rap rages against the "evils" of the white race and a system of sociopolitical oppression and reflects a "ghetto myopia" that is a sad testament to the norm of growing up as a racial minority in inner-city America.

So if an individual does not like or respect the police in the first place, listening to gangsta rap could exacerbate his existing disposition but it would not, in and of itself, induce Howard's attack on Trooper Davidson.

"Is gangster rap music an attempt to promote hatred?" the prosecutor asked me. "Is there any basic difference between the message of hate in gangster rap lyrics and that of charismatic leaders of the KKK, skinheads, and Nazi Germany?"

I found his question especially interesting. The message of hate is universal and transcends the boundaries of race, gender, socioeconomics, religion, politics, or geography, I explained, and the hatred and violence in gangster rap reflect a centuries-old belief in Black America that this country's political structure is racially motivated to keep them as oppressed as possible. That notion underlies the basic foundation of the character of Black America, its strengths and weaknesses alike. In comparison, the hate expressed by white supremacist groups is almost always based on their belief that they are historically, culturally, and genetically superior to those who do not have white skin.

"Do you agree that if this music increased the likelihood... of [Trooper Davidson] being executed...that it is no excuse, it is no justification, nor does it reduce the blameworthiness of anybody who committed the hideous act?"

My unequivocal answer was yes.

Ronald Ray Howard took the stand in his defense and revealed the degree to which gangster rap played a role in his social environment in South Park. He first heard of drive-by shootings through the NWA classic "Fuck tha Police," and the song became so popular, "They started doing it in my 'hood." Howard testified that because of similar songs and films like John Singleton's gritty and powerful *Boyz n the Hood*, the mindset in his community changed; instead of settling disputes mano a mano, young people began to commit drive-by shootings.

Under the questioning of his defense attorney, Howard demonstrated a mastery of gangster rap. Before over a dozen songs were played for the court, he succinctly and accurately described each one, deciphering for the jury some of the street slang used by the rappers. The focus of Howard's defense strategy, however, was Tupac Shakur's 2Pacalypse Now, with an emphasis on the songs with the specific theme of killing cops, like "Soulja's Story."

"What do you know about guns?" Tanner asked him.

"Everything." Howard began carrying a gun at the age of fourteen and testified that in South Park it was common for kids as young as seven to carry guns. There he had access to any kind of firearm he wanted, and he had handled a wide range of them—9mms, .22s, .357s, .45s, MAC-10s, TEC-9s, and AK-47s.

In an interesting exchange with the prosecution, Howard acknowledged putting on different faces to benefit himself and impress others. To his grandmother and friends who were devout Christians, he wrote letters professing his belief in God and asking for His forgiveness. He also attempted to demonstrate remorse for killing Trooper Davidson by writing to his widow, Linda Sue, expressing regret for his actions and asking for her forgiveness. The prosecutor challenged Howard's sincerity toward Mrs. Davidson. "If you're going to be remorseful for something you did and sorry," he said, "doesn't that require you to have a recognition that what you did was wrong?" When

Howard agreed, the prosecutor then exposed his chameleonic nature.

So immersed was Howard in street life that he decorated his jail cell with graffiti, claiming that it gave him a sense of home. That is, the streets. When jail officials denied him access to music, Howard asked his friends to transcribe and bring him rap lyrics when they visited. In an attempt to write his own lyrics, he wrote a semi-autobiographical song called "The Nine or My Mind" in which he referenced his killing of Trooper Davidson:

> Well last night me and my wife had a fight
> I'd rather make money than sit and fuss with my honey
> Pack my bags and grab my gat, making sure the clip
>   is fat
> I'm outta there with a funny ass stare
> Said, "See you later"
> But what I didn't know it was my last goodbye
> See I caught a case
> A murder case with death looking in my face
> Shot a cop and watched him drop
> "Damn," I said, "Why did I have to use my nine?"

The prosecutor asked how Howard could contend that listening to gangster rap music contributed to his admittedly wrong behavior, only to request tapes that consisted of songs with lyrics about killing cops on them while incarcerated. When he asserted that Howard's use of music as a defense for his murderous actions was nothing more than just one of the many faces that he chose to show the jury, Howard insisted that the music had influenced his behavior, and that he continued to ask for it while in jail because he was addicted to it.

On June 8, 1993, after approximately forty minutes of deliberation, the jury of eight men and four women—most of whom were white—rejected Ronald Ray Howard's gangster rap defense and convicted him of the capital murder of Trooper Bill Davidson. A month later, the jury sentenced him to death by lethal injection. But my involvement with this case was not over, although a few years would pass and other testimony would take place.

CHAPTER 18:

TESTIFYIN'

I did not expect Kevin to go to the Ice Cube concert with me. When I went to speak to gangster rappers whose tours brought them to Salt Lake City, he never joined me. "You understand that Black Power stuff," Kevin would say. We rarely discussed race so I understood this as his way of saying, *I'll let you handle that.*

After the concert ended, I approached the door that led backstage. The promoter stepped in to block me. "You can't go in there."

"Sergeant Stallworth, Salt Lake Area Gang Project." I flashed my badge.

He steeled himself in front of the door. "I said you can't go in there."

No one was going to stop me from going backstage to have a conversation with Ice Cube or anyone else. "Get the fuck out of my way," I said. My conviction empowered me to stand up to people far more powerful than this guy, and I was not afraid to use my authority on people who chose to get in my way. "Or I will arrest you for interfering with an officer in the performance of his job."

The promoter stepped aside, and I went backstage. I marched up to Ice Cube's door and knocked. When the door opened, I was met with the glares of Ice Cube's entourage. I scanned the room for Ice, sensing and ignoring the discomfort of his pseudo-gang. He had just come offstage and was holding a bucket of Kentucky Fried Chicken. Without saying a word, Ice held out the bucket to me.

I politely helped myself to a leg and took a bite. "In a few weeks, I'm going to Washington, DC, to testify against the banning of gangsta rap." In between bites of chicken, I explained to Ice Cube that I wanted his input so that my testimony before the Senate committee would be fair and honest. "You're always saying that cops don't listen to you. Well, here is a cop listening to you."

Then I launched into a rap:

Fuck the police comin' straight from the underground
A young nigga got it bad 'cause I'm brown
And not the other color so police think
They have the authority to kill a minority

Ice Cube stood there with his mouth open as this cop rapped his verse to the youth national anthem "Fuck tha

Police" while waving a drumstick. Then he began smiling, his entourage behind him cracking up. Ice Cube motioned for me to have a seat and another piece of chicken. We spent almost an hour discussing gangsta rap, the social conditions that inspired the music, and other topics while finishing off the bucket of KFC.

The invitation to testify before the US Senate came as a surprise and from none other than Senator Carol Moseley Braun herself. During this time, Congress held numerous hearings and floated several bills focused on regulating popular culture in response to the rants of Tipper Gore and C. Delores Tucker about the dangers of profane and violent lyrics. In addition to the recording industry, they took aim at television networks and video game companies. Even Saturday-morning cartoons were under congressional scrutiny. When Moseley Braun's sixteen-year-old son introduced her to a popular underground record on the acid/house scene in her native Chicago called "Beat the Bitch with a Bat," the first African American woman to serve in the US Senate scheduled a hearing before the Senate Committee on the Judiciary's Subcommittee on Juvenile Justice to "examine the effects of violent and demeaning imagery in popular music on American youth" in February 1994. "That's not artistic expression," Senator Moseley Braun told the *Washington Post*. "If we feed them [youth] garbage, it's garbage in, garbage out."

About a year earlier, sensing that the music, culture, and politics of gangster rap had not been adequately explored by law enforcement academia, I had written a twelve-page essay in an attempt to capture my insights on gang culture. When I sent it to the president of the California Gang Investigators Association to get his feedback, "You're onto something," he said. "Pursue this." With that encouragement, I not only expanded that first essay to 116 pages but also wrote a second one about the significant developments in gangster rap music since the Rodney King uprisings.

When I heard about the hearing before the Subcommittee on Juvenile Justice, I sent a copy of my expanded essay to Senator Moseley Braun's office. I never expected a response. Knowing that gangster rap would be a prime target at this hearing, I wanted Congress to understand its historical context and cultural significance. After reviewing my paper, Senator Moseley Braun's office called me. She had determined that I had a unique and knowledgeable point of view to contribute to the hearing and requested that I testify.

To make the most of that opportunity, I knew I had to speak to Ice Cube when he came to perform in Salt Lake City. After my "performance," he said, "I don't think cops knew the lyrics to 'Fuck tha Police.'" He was right about that. Most cops were offended by the title alone and wouldn't give the lyrics a second thought. When I got up to wash my hands before leaving, Ice Cube said, "I've never encountered a cop who took this sort of interest. When we deal with the police in LA, they treat us with disrespect from the get-go. You, though, you approached me like a man, talked to me like a man. You've shown respect for me, and I respect you for that. Thank you."

In my conversation with Ice Cube, he affirmed and

elaborated on my understanding that there was more to the music than the words, "Fuck tha police." We had to know where kids were coming from—their origins, their life stories, their grievances—all of which can be found in these songs. If we banned gangsta rap, not only would we be limiting free speech, we also would be eliminating the key way to comprehend the gangster world. To stop the spread of gang culture across the country, we had to use gangsta rap to understand it. When I was willing to take a step back and listen to the music rather than condemn it, I realized and accepted that I had a responsibility to convince others to do the same. Otherwise, the entire nation would experience the same violence as Los Angeles and Salt Lake City.

Senator Moseley Braun gave me an invitation to do this on a national stage, and I had to decide if I was going to accept it. Recently the highway patrol captain in charge of narcotics had the nerve to say to my face that the highway patrol leadership questioned whether I could be trusted to interact professionally with people in positions of power. They even went so far as to express concern that I might tell a high-ranking official to go fuck themselves or kiss my ass. "If I were to say something like that," I told the captain, "it's because the person deserves it." I knew how to speak professionally to people. I didn't need a babysitter. So upon receiving the invitation to testify at the hearing, I immediately knew my superiors would be unwilling to send me to Washington, DC. Instead they would send someone else—probably a lieutenant—to discuss *my* research and work.

Even when I occasionally crossed the line, I never intended to hurt anyone, and this testimony would be no different. By accepting Senator Moseley Braun's invitation to participate in the hearing, I was not looking to retaliate against my law enforcement colleagues, Utah officials, or anyone else. I wanted to speak truth to those in power on behalf of the kids and families that I had gotten to know well. How far would I go to do the right thing? Not even I could have predicted. Whether they wanted me to or not, I would attend the hearing to protect the state of Utah and the country overall from being overcome by gangs. I was done with others speaking on my behalf, softening my message and downplaying just how dire the threat was. I was no longer allowing anyone to curtail me, and for the sake of this country, I hoped that I was not too late. Sergeant Stallworth was going to Washington, DC.

To summarize the media coverage of the time, February 23, 1994, was the day America put popular music on trial, and one could argue that the key defendant was hip-hop music. The hearing in which I testified was called "Shaping Our Response to Violent and Demeaning Imagery in Popular Music." I was among fifteen witnesses divided across three panels including Congresswoman Maxine Waters, singer Dionne Warwick, and C. Delores Tucker. The only law enforcement officer in the country invited to participate, I gave my statement as part of the first panel, which opened with Tucker. My turn was scheduled before the last speaker, Darryl James, the founder of *Rap Sheet*, and after Michael Eric Dyson, the notoriously prolific and erudite professor and preacher.

Because the audience had erupted in applause several times during Dyson's remarks, Senator Moseley Braun felt the need to admonish it to keep the proceedings at a suitable pace. "I would implore you, let us keep this on a fast track," she said. "And the applause and the like is really not appropriate for a Senate hearing." Then the senator turned to me. "Sergeant Stallworth?"

"Thank you, Ms. Moseley Braun," I said. "First of all, I would like to know who put me after the professor here."

This time instead of applauding, the audience laughed. "I know. It is tough, isn't it?" said Senator Moseley Braun. "That is all right. You have something important to contribute."

And I proceeded to make that contribution. This marked the first of three times I would testify at a congressional hearing. Because these appearances further solidified my reputation as an expert in the correlation between gangsta rap and gang culture, I would also be called to the stand as an expert witness in one of the most significant legal cases in American cultural history.

CHAPTER 19:

HAMMER DIDN'T HURT 'EM

On a Saturday afternoon in late September 1994, Torrance "Torrie" Lambrose bumped into Theodore "Teddy" Davis at Smith's Food and Drug Center. Some say that as kids the seventeen-year-olds had once been friends. That is, until the gang lifestyle came between them.

A member of the Diamond Street Crips, Torrie was wearing a T-shirt memorializing his homey Justin "JP" Raso. A couple of weeks earlier his fellow Crip had been at a party that spilled onto the street just as a member of the North Paw Family Gang walked by with his friends. There were mad-dog stares, name-calling, racial slurs.

And then the handguns came out.

JP and another partygoer were both shot and rushed to LDS Hospital. The other boy was hit in the arm and survived the shooting, but JP died from a bullet to the head. When the police arrested the shooter, he claimed self-defense. After the killing of Justin Raso, the gang unit was out in full force. We responded to reports of drive-bys and broke up parties, intent on squelching acts of retaliation. But then a week later, Torrie ran into Teddy—a Black Mafia Gangster, meaning a North Paw ally—at the checkout line at Smith's.

Teddy said something to Torrie, who remained silent, leaving the store and driving away.

But then he came back. With a .38 revolver in hand, Torrie waited outside for Teddy to exit the store. In a parking lot filled with about twenty other people—including a carload of kids—the friends turned rivals engaged in a shootout reminiscent of a Hollywood western. Torrie fired a volley of rounds from the revolver while Teddy got off at least one shot from a .380 semiautomatic. That shot was all it took. Despite being mortally wounded, Torrie managed to chase down Teddy in the parking lot and fire one more round into his head.

Both gang members died between two parked cars, "their bodies touching, their blood soaking each other's clothing," as the *Deseret News* reported it. When police responded to the scene, they found relatives of the victims hurling insults at one another across the lot. The bodies of both boys lay on the ground for over two hours.

Several weeks after the tragedy, Torrance Lambrose's stepfather Paul Foreman discovered a rap tape among his possessions. Believing the lyrics may have contributed to Torrie's premature death, he contacted the office of Salt Lake City mayor Margaret "Deedee" Corradini, the first woman elected to that office. She invited both Torrie's and Teddy's families to meet with her, according to the *Deseret News,* to discuss ideas for preventing gang violence. Overcome with grief over the deaths of their sons, neither mother attended, but Mayor Corradini did meet with Foreman and two other loved ones. At that meeting, Foreman gave her the cassette.

The tragic shootout rocked Salt Lake City, and many in the community feared that the rivalry between Diamond Street and BMG would escalate into a brutal gang war. It captured political attention, which further fueled the media frenzy. Three days after the shootout, Governor Mike Leavitt held a press conference in which he unveiled a series of reactive initiatives including but not limited to ordering double-bunking at youth detention facilities, demanding that the courts speed up the certification of youth as adult offenders, and—the most ludicrous response of all—dispatching a dozen highway patrol troopers to work in Salt Lake City. Mayor Corradini welcomed this support.

When Foreman gave the mayor the rap album he found among Torrie's things, she also rushed to publicly express outrage at the explicit tales of alcohol and drug use and dealing, graphic sex and violence, and cop killings. This was the same person who hired a police chief whose response to gangs was to enlist SWAT. Corradini was a major proponent of expanding the number of juvenile facilities and locking up more kids. Suspecting that her reactions to the cassette Foreman gave was presumptuous, I arranged to meet with her.

I began our conversation by asking the mayor if she had listened to any of the songs on Lambrose's tape. My experience with Utah leaders taught me I could not assume this. "No, my staff did," she admitted. "But I am convinced that this particular tape was directly responsible for the deaths of those young men. Those two boys are dead because one of them was listening to this music." Then Mayor Corradini wasted no time in revealing her agenda. "I want to address the negative influence of gangster rap music by organizing a nationwide boycott through the US Conference of Mayors."

To say I was amused by the mayor's ill-informed outrage and her futile plans would be an understatement. Such an impulsive reaction demanded a blunt reality check. "Organizing a national boycott would not be a wise move on your part, Mayor," I warned her. As a police sergeant working for the state, I could have been intimidated to challenge the most powerful person in Salt Lake City's government, but I was confident in my expertise—which was getting acknowledged nationwide—so I did not mince words. The stakes were too high. "In my capacity as the Utah gang intelligence coordinator, I am considered the foremost law enforcement authority on gangsta rap music in this country, and if you go down this road, you will be putting a target on yourself, Salt Lake City, and Utah. You will be labeled an extremist prude, an anti-Black racist, and a cultural elitist." As I spoke, Mayor Corradini gave me a long, hard stare. I was determined to proceed but lowered the tension by posing another question. "Who's the rapper on the cassette tape?"

"MC Hammer." Then she showed me the cassette. If you're a hip-hop connoisseur, you understand why this made me chuckle.

Although he had released *The Funky Headhunter* earlier that year with an edgier look and sound than his previous albums, Hammer was still largely known and loved for being "too legit to quit." Today rap aficionados are aware that the same artist who danced the Typewriter in glittery harem pants across our screen to the major crossover hit "U Can't Touch This" was regarded by his peers in both the recording industry and on the streets of his native Oakland as beyond a certified gangster. However, to the public at large in the early 1990s, Hammer was in no way a progenitor of gangsta rap music. On the contrary, *The Funky Headhunter* peaked at No. 2 on Billboard's R&B chart, and the most controversial cut on the album, "Pumps and a Bump," made headlines not because of gangster-oriented lyrics but because of its sexually provocative music video that featured Hammer in a Speedo.

I tried to reason with Mayor Corradini. "Gangsta rap exists, and some of it is vulgar and violent," I conceded. "But do you think white music artists have never advocated for violence in their songs? Are you prepared, Mayor, to also promote a boycott of country music with its outlaw musings on drugs, drunkenness, violent conflict, and gun culture?" Then I appealed to her political expediency. "I think it would damage your reputation to defend one violent music genre popular with a large segment of the white population while simultaneously attacking another one popular with young people of color."

Mayor Corradini would not be swayed. "Something needs to be done to prevent future tragedies such as this, and I feel so strongly that those two boys would still be alive were it not for the violent messages in this music. They were obviously influenced by the violent imagery of this and also like-minded movies."

"But you just admitted that you did not listen to the tape. How would you know what the tone or messages of the songs were?"

"A police officer told me that album was of the gangsta rap genre."

"This is *not* gangsta rap," I said, no longer able to contain my dismay. "And MC Hammer is not now and has never been considered a gangster rapper."

Without saying a word, the mayor pointed to the album cover of Hammer kneeling while wearing a black skullcap, a black tank top, and sunglasses. In her defense, to a person who knew nothing about gang culture, he might look like a gang member. But to someone who professionally studied gangs, this was akin to concluding Michael Jackson was a gang member based on the cover art of his album *Bad*.

It was laughable.

But I did not laugh long. The mayor's ignorance at best was counterproductive; if fed with political ambition, it could potentially be dangerous. Since I had her attention, I had to keep trying to educate her. "There are certain characteristics unique to gangster rap music. Graphic imagery of street life punctuated with profane references to male or female anatomy and explicit sexuality..." I explained. "*The Funky Headhunter* has none of this." I even added that Hammer's attempt to rebrand himself was perceived as an attempt to cash in on the popularity of gangsta rap and had cost him significant fans and record sales.

Ignoring my point, Mayor Corradini declared, "I'm also calling for a boycott of gang movies." She specifically cited *Juice, Menace II Society, Above the Rim,* and even *Boyz n the Hood,* which in 1991 had made writer-director the late John Singleton the youngest and first African American to be nominated for an Academy Award for best director.

"Why are you pursuing a suppression effort against movies made by and about inner-city Black youth?" I asked. The mayor's proposed "advocacy" was nothing other than an elitist attack on Black cultural art, and I had to call it out.

"Because I don't like the violence and drug use promoted in those movies," she said. "Movies like these contribute to violent teen behavior by promoting that violence, promiscuity, and alcohol and substance abuse are normal."

"Have you seen any of the movies you just mentioned?"

I already knew the answer. "No." Again, rather than watching the films herself, the mayor was "made aware" of their alleged content by staff members who had claimed to have watched them.

With a deliberate edge to my voice, I leaned forward and said, "I find your position to be racist." The mayor's face dropped. "You've falsely labeled dance music as gangsta rap. And if negative messages in movies are so threatening to the well-being of youth, why do so many westerns glorify John Wayne, a self-admitted white supremacist? Why do so many depict Native Americans as violent, savage terrorists intent on destroying innocent white settlers who were, in fact, perpetrators of Native American genocide? With all due respect, Mayor, you have little to no insight on cultural matters unique to the minority community.

"Are you going to defend the violence in the *Rambo* roles of Sylvester Stallone? The *Die Hard* series of Bruce Willis? The *Terminator* series of Arnold Schwarzenegger—who by the way executed thirty police officers in its opening scene? How about mob movies like the Oscar-winning *Godfather* series; the Oscar-winning *Untouchables* in which Robert De Niro beats a man to death with a baseball bat; *Taxi Driver* again with De Niro; *Goodfellas*; *Scarface* starring Al Pacino? The Clint Eastwood *Dirty Harry* series, and the martial arts movies of Chuck Norris, Steven Seagal, and Jean-Claude Van Damme? The slasher movies like *Nightmare on Elm Street*, *Halloween*, and *Friday the 13th*? None of these was by or about Black people."

I then schooled Mayor Corradini how the most glorified act of gang violence—the drive-by shooting—was first depicted in the 1960s on the television series *The Untouchables*. "The cultural elite such as yourself never criticize the criminal pathology exhibited by Italian, Irish, and Jewish criminals—all white—routinely represented in those storylines the same way you so casually demonize young Blacks for theirs."

Not only did Mayor Corradini scoff, she doubled down. "I want to ban rap concerts at any Salt Lake City–owned venue," she said, "and appeal to music and video stores to stop marketing merchandise with overtones of gang violence."

By the end of our meeting, the mayor reluctantly agreed not to pursue her boycott against gangster rap and gang-oriented movies, but I left convinced she had not considered a single word I'd said. On the contrary, it seemed the more I spoke, the more elaborate her agenda became. But I convinced her. Deedee Corradini never called for a boycott.

I learned later that in her meeting with Torrie Lambrose's family, they had considered organizing a banquet to convene the rival gangs and broker peace between them. Deeming it too risky, however, they abandoned that idea. Foreman continued to claim gangsta rap had been a factor in the young men's deaths, but he also named other causes for the tragic loss of his stepson: the physical bullying that made him drop out of school at fourteen and the alleged failure of the school districts and juvenile courts to compel his return; laws that prohibit young teens from holding jobs and lack of work opportunities and structured environments for those who drop out of school; the leniency of the juvenile justice system that allowed Torrie to continue committing increasingly serious offenses without significant consequences; and, of course, the lure of gangs.

CHAPTER 20:

GANGSTA RAP ON TRIAL

After both my sons had gone to bed, I settled in the living room with my Sony Walkman and yellow legal pad. I slipped on the headphones and pressed PLAY on the first song on my list— "Trapped," the second track on Tupac's debut album *2Pacalypse Now*. As I listened to Tupac rhyme, I captured his opening lines on my legal pad. I paused, rewound, and then replayed the snippet, only moving to the next line when I was satisfied that I had captured his lyrics as accurately as possible. If I had any doubt whatsoever about a specific lyric, I either left it blank or put a question mark in its place. Play, pause, write, replay, repeat. Working from 10:00 p.m. until about 2:00 in the morning, it took me four hours to transcribe the entire song, and I had three more to do before I could take the stand as an expert witness for the second time in the case that put gangsta rap on trial.

Soon after Ronald Ray Howard's conviction in the summer of 1993, the widow of the slain trooper, Linda Sue Davidson, moved forward with a civil lawsuit against Tupac Shakur and his distributor Time Warner as well as Interscope Records, East West Records America, and Atlantic Records Group. It charged that the defendants "[were] grossly negligent in recording, producing, manufacturing, distributing and selling the cassette tape" and therefore liable for the death of Trooper Bill Davidson. "Our goal is to punish Time Warner and wake up the executives who run the music business. This suit isn't just about some storyteller spouting militant rhetoric here. 2Pac is dangerously serious," said her attorney Jim Cole. "This suit is about stopping giant corporations from shamelessly making money off music designed to incite impressionable young men to shoot and kill cops like Bill."

When arguments in the civil lawsuit finally began in October 1995, I once again was asked to testify as an expert witness, this time for the plaintiff. I immediately recognized it as a landmark case with potential ramifications for the protection of free speech. The album *2Pacalypse Now* was called "obscene" and said to contain "fighting words [that] defames peace officers like Officer Davidson" and "tends to incite imminent, illegal conduct on the part of individuals like Howard." Davidson's attorneys argued that the defendants were liable for "producing violent music that proximately caused the death of Officer Davidson."

"This is a First Amendment issue," I told Jim Cole.

He assured me, "We have no intention of crusading against the First Amendment."

But I stood firm in my position that they did not have a case because the music was not the cause of Trooper David-son's death. "You're not going to win," I said. While I acknowl-edged that community outrage might score them a temporary win in the lower court, the defendants ultimately would appeal and prevail. "The federal court that's deciding this case is not going to trample the First Amendment." I also made it clear that while I was willing to help the court understand the con-tent of the music and its significance to those who listen to it, I would neither state that the music was responsible for Howard's actions nor attack a Black cultural art form.

And Linda Sue Davidson herself was very apprehensive about my involvement. When I met her, she was angry—angry that this Black man had killed her husband and angry that this Black man was trying to help. She admitted that she had res-ervations about me, and I told her that I understood how she felt. We discussed it further, and Linda Sue became more com-fortable with me. "I'm doing this on behalf of my husband and children," she said, starting to come around. "If you can help me, I would be most appreciative."

They were determined to proceed with the lawsuit against Time Warner, and as much as I supported the constitutional right to freedom of expression, I also believed that Trooper Davidson's wife and children deserved to get any money they could. Despite facing the death penalty for killing a member of law enforcement, Howard's jailhouse lyrics lacked intro-spection about his actions and instead revealed a destructive impulse steeped in homicide, drugs, and misogyny. "To me this case is an effort in futility, but I will try to help you collect the money." With no expectation or desire for compensation, I agreed to decipher four specific songs on *2Pacalypse Now* that referenced killing cops, including "Souljah's Story."

Developed for my presentations to police audiences, my transcription process was detailed and tedious. Cops claimed they did not listen to rap music because the heavy bass made it difficult for them to understand what the artists were saying, so my approach eliminated the percussion and immersed them with pure lyrics. But first I had to transcribe the songs, and this time the stakes were much higher. For Davidson's lawsuit against Tupac, Time Warner, et al., it took me sixteen hours—four per song—to transcribe the lyrics I was asked to analyze so I could feel confident in my ability to enter a courtroom, raise my hand on a Bible, and testify to their meaning. When I lectured to police groups, I offered my interpretations of metaphors and otherwise put the meaning of lyrics into context, but here I wrote down what I heard word for word. Because transcriptions are for court purposes, I had to remain literal.

I already was familiar with Tupac's music before I prepared my testimony for the civil lawsuit against him, and my first impression of him had been, *He's just another rapper.* I figured all rappers were essentially saying the same thing albeit in a different way, infusing their songs with their own creative style. But then I listened more closely to Tupac's lyrics and realized this artist was different from his peers. As I paid greater attention to him and learned of his upbringing as a Black Panther baby, his words made more sense to me.

Two songs in particular had changed my opinion about Tupac: "Dear Mama" and "Brenda's Got a Baby." This kid was communicating his love for his mother despite her crack addiction and his hope for her betterment. In "Brenda's Got a Baby," Tupac was expressing heartfelt feelings toward a young woman in a difficult predicament with the men who abandoned her.

I thought, *This kid is brilliant.*

Now that he's achieved the iconic status of entertainers such as Elvis Presley and Marilyn Monroe, many details about Tupac Shakur's experiences and perspectives are known to scholars and fans alike almost thirty years later through countless books and documentaries. At the height of his popularity in the early 1990s, however, I learned more about his personal life and artistic objectives from a little-known five-hundred-page deposition he gave for the Time Warner lawsuit fifteen months before his untimely death in a drive-by shooting on the Las Vegas Strip. It struck me how in high school, he was the outsider who was bullied by members of street gangs because he dressed like a hippie and couldn't play basketball, retreating into himself, reading Shakespeare, and writing poetry. Inspired by *The Autobiography of Malcolm X* and the activism of his mother, Black Panther Afeni Shakur, when the opportunity came for him to become a solo artist, Tupac chose to create political music that would contribute to a social movement of underdogs, have-nots, and even thugs.

"The thugs are the only ones who backed me up when the police was after me...that's who I'm talking to," Tupac said.

"Wasn't no positive brothers coming to help me when my ass was getting kicked."

This begged the question of whether Tupac Shakur truly hated the police to the extent described in his lyrics. He expressed an admiration for cops who put their lives on the line to serve their communities but also described personal experiences with police brutality and likened law enforcement to street gangs. "The biggest gang isn't the Bloods and Crips. It's the police. They wear colors, they stick together, they lie together." Tupac even relayed an incident of brutality while he was incarcerated. "I got attacked and smacked and choked in this prison right here, pulled out of my cell. And the one thing they kept repeating was, 'We are the biggest gang in New York state. Not you. We are.'"

I empathized not only with his thirst for knowledge but also with the disillusion that came from its pursuit as a Black man in America. When Tupac wrote in "Words of Wisdom," "No Malcolm X in my history text / Why is that? / Because he tried to educate and liberate all Blacks," it echoed my own political awakening as a young boy growing up in El Paso, Texas. I became an avid student of American history, especially of the efforts of the Founding Fathers to establish a nation free of British tyranny. During high school, I had developed a great admiration and respect specifically for Abraham Lincoln. I read anything and everything about the Great Emancipator of my ancestors. Not until years after I graduated and continued studying independently did I learn that despite opposing slavery as an abhorrent institution, Lincoln essentially regarded

Blacks as adult children who were inferior to whites and not deserving of full equality with them.

Tupac had been educated as a child that the police only liked Black people who kept their heads down and submitted to their authority and that no Black male with the last name Shakur made it past the age of fifteen without being killed or jailed. And yet he also spoke of the futility of violence toward police, despite occasions of justification, in a frustrated but nuanced way. "When you strike back at the police, you die. You don't have a chance. It's a trick, it's a trap, it's a vicious cycle," he testified. "Everybody in my story that ever fought the police died, went to jail or something bad happened to them. There are no good stories in here about people who fought the police, good or bad, and got away."

As part of his deposition, Tupac was asked to recite and interpret numerous songs. In what I took as an example of his artistic integrity, he refused to answer questions about lyrics in his songs that he personally had not written. Some of the lyric sheets he read into the official record were transcribed by me. When asked if they were a reasonably accurate transcription, he stated, "It's accurate as far as somebody listening to the tapes, this is what you would hear. But some of the words, what they sound like are not what they actually are, but it's close enough." Tupac did not offer any corrections to my transcriptions of his lyrics.

When I took the stand in *Davidson v. Time Warner, Inc.*, I testified for three hours. In my testimony, I reiterated the points I had made in the criminal trial regarding the street gang subculture and the gangster mentality, offered my analysis of the songs I had transcribed and made connections to Howard's upbringing and lifestyle. But I refused to provide a blanket condemnation of him or testify that the music caused him to kill Trooper Davidson.

Davidson's attorney presented numerous arguments to the US District Court for the Southern District of Texas. First, the creators of 2Pacalypse Now should have reasonably foreseen the harm that could result from its distribution; Tupac Shakur's words were "'a call to battle' against police and an incitement to shoot any police officer who stops or detains gangstas (a known violent subculture to whom gangsta rap is primarily directed and marketed)." They also cited two cases against Soldier of Fortune as precedent in which both the US District Court and Federal Court of Appeals held the magazine liable for advertisements soliciting criminal activities that had led to injury and death. As for the free speech defense, Davidson's attorneys claimed that "the First Amendment does not protect expression that is directed to inciting or producing imminent lawless action and is likely to incite or produce such action." They further contended that 2Pacalypse Now was not subject to First Amendment protection because the album was libelous and defamatory to law enforcement officers; its "lyrics impeach the honesty, integrity, virtue and reputation of law enforcement officers, including Officer Davidson, by stating that police officers are crooked and attempt to frame Black men [the song "Violent"], harass and brutalize ["Trapped"], and kill them without reason ["Soulja's Story"]. These attacks on their reputations expose the officers to public hatred, contempt and ridicule among those who are exposed to the raps from the album, and particularly among the gangsta subculture."

We had to wait until 1997 for the ultimate outcome in Linda Sue Davidson's civil suit against Time Warner, Inc. In the interim, more cases emerged throughout the country in which defendants assumed the "rap defense" so the verdict had major repercussions for both freedom of expression and criminal justice. Having offered my expertise to the national discourse, I returned to my main focus and immediate sphere of influence—the gang problem in the state of Utah.

Ironically, that meant going back to Washington, DC.

CHAPTER 21:

MR. STALLWORTH GOES TO WASHINGTON AGAIN

O ver the years, my conflict with the Clearfield Job Corps had grown increasingly heated and public because I had no qualms about challenging the polished image its leadership presented. When I told the local media that Crips and Bloods street gangs were using Job Corp centers throughout the country as pipelines into new drug markets, the Clearfield director Don Myrtle missed the forest for the trees, claiming it was unreasonable to expect hard-core gang members to enroll in their program when it only paid a $40-per-month stipend, and they could make thousands on the street. Over my years in Utah, the executive director of the Clearfield Job Corps would change, but the denial would persist.

Clearfield chief of police Daren Green was complicit in the denial. He insisted that having a "gang mental set" did not mean a student was a gang member. Even when he conceded to the *Deseret News* that it was possible that Clearfield Job Corps students might visit Salt Lake City or Ogden on the weekends, meet with gang contacts, and pass on drug trafficking information, Green said, "That's no different than a student coming from L.A. on a vacation and doing the same thing."

I discovered how deep the politics in Clearfield ran—from organizational leaders to city officials—when the organization offered me a job. Putting its critics on the payroll was a common tactic the Job Corps used to compromise them. Nothing fancy, just a way to make a little extra money but enough to buy your silence. I could not be bought, however.

And I had the evidence. Because Job Corps refused to share data with me about their participants, I carried out an informal survey on the streets of Ogden and Salt Lake City with students on weekend pass from the Clearfield campus. Almost three hundred gang members themselves volunteered which sets they represented—twenty-nine Crip gangs, twenty-one Blood gangs, seven Hispanic gangs with roots in Los Angeles, and two major gang factions, the Vice Lords and the Black Gangster Disciples, who hailed from Illinois.

Then in January 1995, I seized a speaking opportunity to enlist a national ally in my ongoing clash with the Clearfield Job Corps. The Job Corps had been under scrutiny and in danger of elimination for at least a decade before I testified before the Senate. President Reagan had proposed to eliminate federal funding to the high-cost program (the $14,000 it cost per student in 1985 would be almost $40,000 today—the same as the average cost of tuition at a private college). None other than Utah senator Orrin Hatch had used his leverage as the ranking Republican on the Senate Labor and Human Resources Committee to save the program. Then about 1993, Republicans had defeated the Clinton administration's attempt to increase the number of centers from 113 to 163. Two years later, believing that for decades the Job Corps "had tolerated unacceptable behavior in the interest of keeping up the numbers," Kansas senator Nancy Landon Kassebaum, chair of the Committee on Labor and Human Resources, launched an investigation into the effectiveness—or lack thereof—of the Job Corps program and its continued congressional funding. Upon learning about this hearing, I made the trip to Washington, DC, to testify, hoping to embolden Utah officials take a more aggressive stance against the Job Corps's duplicity.

I opened my testimony with my overall support for the Job Corps as a vital endeavor that gave the "have-nots" means to elevate themselves, which in turn bettered our society. To gain the positive benefits of social programs like the Job Corps, however, we had to control gang culture, which was spreading like social bacteria beyond inner cities and infecting children as young as six. I contrasted the privately run Clearfield center and the other local Job Corps in Weber Basin, which was managed by the Department of Labor and cooperated with law enforcement. In fact, I proposed that private management of a public initiative resulted in a Frankenstein monster that had to be held accountable to the taxpayers who funded it yet were negatively impacted by the criminal element it had imported into their communities. I specifically described the "brick wall of defiant excuses" the Salt Lake Area Gang Project faced whenever I sought information from the Clearfield Job Corps about the gang presence at its center that had bled over into our communities, only to be told, "We don't have gang members out here. We have gang wannabes."

"Sergeant Stallworth, if all of a sudden, you were a member of the US Senate, and you could do anything you wanted to do to deal with the gang problem, what would you be doing?" asked Senator Paul Simon from Illinois.

"That's a dangerous question to ask me," I said. I was making a joke and telling the truth. The latter became evident when I returned from Washington and was confronted by several people who felt threatened by the testimony I gave that day.

In response to Senator Simon's question, I testified that I believed unequivocally in our young people and refused to give up on them. "The vast majority of these kids who are involved in gangs and causing the problems which are epidemic in this country are really good kids," I said. "They are confused kids. They are at a stage in their lives where they are revolting against something, and in many cases, they do not know what they are revolting against.

"I liken it to the time when I was growing up in the 1970s, and we had the Vietnam War, we had all the protests that were going on and so on. But we had something we could attach ourselves to, and when we went through that rebellious stage, we latched onto it, and whether we were right or wrong was not the issue; it was an issue for us, and we latched onto it. Kids today do not have that, and a lot of these kids, especially in my state, are looking for something to revolt against, there is nothing, and this gang issue is the big thing. They latch onto it, and they do not know what they are getting themselves into, and if we do not act quickly, we will lose them; they literally get lost."

But if Senator Simon had asked ten different people who worked with gangs, he would have received ten different answers to his question. My response was that while the Job Corps could be beneficial to young people if it were properly managed, we needed additional social programs including alternative education for those who were not cut out for college but still desired to have well-paying jobs and raise a family.

I also criticized the private management of Job Corps sites like the Clearfield campus, which was run by the Management and Training Corporation, and even called for the federal government to consider a comprehensive investigation into the program's administration, including closer examination of the statistics it generated as proof of social return on the public funding invested. "Is the program having a positive effect on the vast number of its participants," I asked, "or are the statistics reflecting a financial boondoggle that could be better used in a different format?" I closed my testimony by submitting into the public record the results of my informal survey and a report I wrote for the 1993 Utah Governor's Summit on Gang Violence. The report devoted fifteen pages to the role the Job Corps played in the state's gang problem, including a partial list of crimes involving Clearfield students that had warranted a police response over the years.

After I gave my testimony, the late brother-in-law of John and Robert Kennedy, R. Sargent Shriver Jr., came toward me. I presume all politicians are a bunch of pretentious pricks. White, Black, Democratic, Republican, it doesn't matter to me. They'll cheat, lie, and steal to get your vote. But I was honored to meet Shriver because of his political history and association with President Kennedy. I was in elementary school when JFK came through El Paso. They dismissed us early because his route from the airport to the downtown hotel went past my school, walking us to the corner of a major intersection where we waited for him. The crowd kept swelling, and I kept inching toward the curb determined to see the president. Then his motorcade came down the street, and as it slowly passed, I saw this pink-faced man standing up and waving at the crowd. You could recognize John Kennedy a mile away because of his smile. I also remember seeing Vice President Lyndon B. Johnson and then governor John Connally. The light changed, the presidential limousine drove off, and I walked four blocks home, satisfied to have seen such an important public figure whom I had only read about in my history books. This had been a milestone moment in my young life—the first time (although not the last) I would see a US president in person.

Under President Kennedy, Shriver had been the director of the Peace Corps—of which the Job Corps was an offshoot. He was gracious with me. As he shook my hand, Shriver thanked me for my honesty about the Job Corps and my commitment to young people.

As he walked away, an unfamiliar gentleman approached me. When I accepted his extended hand, he said, "I'm Bob Marquardt." I immediately knew who he was, why he was in Washington, DC, and what he thought of what I had told the Senate committee. Marquardt was the founder of the Management and Training Corporation, the largest operator of Job Corps programs in the nation, including the Clearfield campus. MTC received millions in federal dollars. Marquardt and I had never formally met, but I was aware of the negative things he said about me because of my public criticism of the Job Corps. "Why did you have to say those things to the committee?" he asked me. By the firmness of Marquardt's grip and the tone of his voice, I was supposed to be intimidated.

I was not. "Because it was the truth."

"That is all well and good," he said, "but why did you have to *say* it?"

"My testimony was based on the facts my colleagues and I in the gang unit have experienced," I replied firmly. "Nothing was fabricated. Would you rather that I gave false testimony to the committee?"

"That is beside the point," Marquardt said with an air of haughty superiority. "Why was it necessary for you to say it to the senators on the committee?"

"Because I swore an oath to tell the truth, and I honored that oath. Would you have me promote the lie that the Job Corps projects to the public and in congressional hearings?"

I grew tired of this verbal charade with a corrupt bureaucrat. "Everything I said in my testimony was based on facts, and I am willing to debate them with you in any public forum you choose. Are you willing to take me up on my offer?"

Marquardt obviously was unaccustomed to getting challenged. I, on the other hand, was well accustomed to challenging people who were unaccustomed to getting challenged. "We'll just see about that," he huffed before storming off.

Through their aides, both Utah senators Robert Bennett and Orrin Hatch requested meetings with me before I left Washington, and I accepted. While it was routine for congressional officials to request private meetings and photo ops with constituents visiting the Capitol, I knew the senators had the same agenda as Marquardt: to censure my criticism of the local Job Corps and silence me. I already had met Hatch once before and did not like him.

The chief of police of Salt Lake City once called a meeting in his office while Hatch was in town. Even though I was not in a leadership position, he invited me to attend because of my role in the gang effort. I was sitting among police chiefs and sheriffs when in walked the senator. The chief introduced him, and Hatch made his way around the room, putting on that politician face and shaking everyone's hand. "Hello. How are you doing? Hey, I know you!" When he reached me, he took my hand and said, "Oh, I'm very familiar with you."

"Who am I?" I asked.

Silence. "Well, I know we've talked before."

"No, sir, we haven't." *What a pretentious little prick.* I didn't like Hatch because he'd pretended to be a native Utahn when he had moved to Salt Lake City from Pennsylvania to run for the available Senate seat. *You don't know me,* I thought as he pumped my hand. *You never talked to half the people in this room before today.*

Hatch's aide escorted me into his office. After greeting me with that phony smile and platitudes about how pleased he was to meet me, he made his position obvious. "I am a little concerned about your testimony today. Job Corps is a financial and economic concern to Clearfield and the State of Utah," Hatch said. "You should be aware of the importance and power of your words and how they can impact an issue."

In other words, the program brought too much federal money into the local economy, and I should shut up about Clearfield. How could such influential elected officials use that as an excuse to turn their back on the high cost—both financially and socially—the gang members at the Clearfield Job Corps were exacting on Utahn citizens? I had taken an oath to serve and protect them from gang influences, and the pressure tactics of these powerful politicians pissed me off.

I braced myself for the fallout of my Washington testimony when I returned to Salt Lake City. After all, if the highest-ranking elected officials in Utah suggest you not do your job, all the others at the statewide level feel emboldened to push you around. Or try to. Whenever I testified before Congress, I did so on my own time and dime even though I considered this additional work an integral part of my job. I used my vacation time and paid for the trips to Washington—the flight, hotel room, meals and incidentals, everything—out of my own pocket. I would fly east on a Thursday, testify on a Friday morning, and board a plane back to Utah that same night.

About the time I began providing expert testimony, I lost one of my few allies when Kevin was transferred out of the gang unit in 1994. We had different personalities yet complementary approaches to the job. He was a willing and capable yin to my yang, providing a calm, soothing alternative to my irascible nature. Where I was demonstrative and vocal, Kevin was relatively quiet and mellow in his dealings with people. While I would easily launch into a litany of four-letter words at those who verbally attacked me, Kevin rarely allowed a curse word to escape his lips. The rare time he described a particular gang member who was a pain in our collective butts as a "fucker" prompted an incredulous look from me. Kevin just smiled and sheepishly said, "Well, he is."

No matter the issue at hand, he always had my back.

Kevin and I had been partners since 1989, and not only were we effective as partners, but we enjoyed working with each other. But as I've mentioned, police departments are backward facing, and they will reassign someone simply because they believe they have been in a position long enough. It may seem sensible to have kept Kevin and me together, but police departments do not think logically. They irrationally decide that it's time for you to move on and for someone else to get a chance.

And sometimes these decisions are political. The new lieutenant in charge of the gang unit, Sam Shipman, didn't like me, and I hated his guts. He resented that I was a state cop assigned to the Salt Lake City Police Department over whom he had no authority—a "lowly" sergeant in a supervisory capacity that he outranked no less.

His first day on the job, Shipman set out to undermine my authority as a sergeant with a squad in his own right. He called a meeting of all the investigators—we had about ten by then—and announced that from that point forward I would answer to the Salt Lake City sergeant. *That ain't happening*, I thought, but I kept my cool during the meeting. At that point in my tenure as the state's gang intelligence coordinator, any cop in Utah who received gang training got it either directly from me or from someone I had trained, including the sergeant that Shipman expected me to report to. When the meeting ended, I went directly to the deputy chief of police of the Salt Lake City Police Department. He had come to value my judgment, understanding that when I said something about gangs, I knew what I was talking about. The next day I arrived at work, and Shipman called another meeting to "revise" the orders he had issued the previous day. There would be two squads; one would report to the Salt Lake City sergeant and the other would be led by Stallworth. The deputy chief clearly had gotten in touch with Shipman and told him to cut the bullshit.

We never got along after that, and I never trusted him. Because I was a state cop, Shipman could not do anything to me, but he reassigned Kevin and got a new sergeant—none other than former SWAT officer Clark Myers.

Law enforcement also believes the focus of a police department is a uniform division. If someone is transferred from a

plainclothes assignment, they're likely to be put back in uniform for a spell to get acclimated. This policy is essentially why
I left Colorado Springs: I didn't want to go back into uniform.
Kevin initially returned to uniform duty before he was placed
on the investigation squad. He didn't want to go but he had no
say in the matter, and I lost a trusted confidant. I told no one in
the department about my trips to Washington, DC, but given
the nature of my testimony against the Clearfield Job Corps, I
had no doubts that my colleagues and superiors would find out
and take issue.

Sure enough, three days after I testified, I was inundated
with phone calls—everyone from my direct supervisor to the
governor's office.

I had barely sat at my desk that Monday morning when my
captain called. *Here we go.* "Sergeant Stallworth." *You've upset
these people, and now they have to get their five ounces of blood
out of it.*

"Why did you go to Washington?" he asked. I knew my
first transgression was not seeking permission to testify. If I had
done that, the state Department of Public Safety would have
denied approval only to send a highway patrolman whose only
police experience was traffic stops to testify.

"Because it's my right," I said. The trooper culture at DPS
was that you didn't sneeze unless you were given permission to
sneeze. Fuck you, I sneeze whenever I want to. "I'm an American citizen, and I wanted to speak with my representative."

Then the director of the Clearfield Job Corps called me.
After demanding to know why I'd criticized his program at the

Senate hearing, he threatened me. "If you do not stop saying those things about Job Corps," he said, "you will leave me no choice but to go after your job."

"I'll take my message directly to the media and expose your corrupt program for the lie it is, my career be damned! And fuck you." Then I hung up, wondering who they were going to throw at me next.

I had my answer in five minutes when I received yet another call from an MTC executive named Ron Russell. Ron also happened to be my former boss. Not only had I reported to him at the north division of the Narcotics and Liquor Law Enforcement Bureau, but he had recruited me from the Wyoming Division of Criminal Investigation.

"Hi, Ron," he said. "I understand you had an interesting conversation with the Job Corps director."

"I did, and I assume he sent you to try and convince me to do his and MTC's bidding."

Ron chuckled. "Yeah, he thought I might be able to talk to you about this." After those first couple of calls, I appreciated the levity.

"Let me ask you something," I said. "If you were still working for DPS and found yourself being confronted with some pissant bureaucrat trying to intimidate you with threats against your job, what would you have done?"

He hesitated. "I would have probably told them the same thing that you did."

"Exactly. So give the Job Corps director and Bob Marquardt a personal message from me. Tell them to *fuck off*!"

Ten minutes after that call ended, my lieutenant called. I had already butted heads with him several years earlier. I was preparing my 1993 biennial statewide report on gangs when my lieutenant had ordered me to delete a section that contained a reference to the historical presence of the KKK in Utah, claiming it was too provocative to include. At a subsequent encounter I had with the governor of Utah, I asked him to sign the cover page of the report. When I submitted it to my lieutenant, I told him that the governor's signature, in essence, made that report a historical document that could not be altered in any way. He was not pleased with that, he was not pleased when I refused to quell my public statements about the Clearfield Job Corps's role in the state's gang problem, and he was not pleased on that Monday morning. "Why is the captain calling me about some remarks you made about the Clearfield Job Corps at a congressional hearing?" This traffic cop I had to answer to was calling me about my trip to Washington while sitting in the office next to mine. (Later when the department issued cell phones, we would argue because he would badger me to text him when I was four steps away and wanted to talk to him in person.)

The phone rang all morning, and I suspected that Bob Marquardt was behind it. He was a powerful businessman in Utah who gave major donations and had many political connections. The verbal sparring with my superiors, past and present, reached a crescendo when I received a direct call from Doug Bodrero, the commissioner of public safety.

A lot of people in the department did not like Doug, but he and I had a good working relationship, and I always found him easy to talk to. He had created the position of gang intelligence coordinator just for me and gave me the freedom to do my job. Whenever my take on an issue was unpopular with the law enforcement community and generated controversy, Doug always gave me the opportunity to explain my position, and whether or not he agreed with me, he would have my back. He had probably been inundated with as many calls as I had that morning, so I could not assume that this time would be no different.

"Why am I getting calls from the governor and Senator Hatch's office telling me that your comments at a Senate hearing on Job Corps represent a threat to the Utah economy?"

I explained, including the confrontation with Bob Marquardt in Washington, DC, the Job Corps director's threat to my job, and the explicit suggestion by the state's two senators that I stop telling the truth about the Job Corps's contribution to Utah's gang problem. Then Doug reiterated what I already knew—the senators as well as the governor viewed my testimony as a threat to Utah's economic outlook because of the much-needed boost the state received in federal funding via the Job Corps program. "If you were to schedule a public forum about the Job Corps's gang influence on Utah society and invited their director to debate me, he wouldn't accept the invitation," I said, standing my ground. "He knows that I have the facts to support my position, and that he doesn't have any to prove his."

After a little more discussion, Doug ultimately dismissed any further concerns. He did urge me to be cognizant of the effect of my public comments on the body politic. "Make sure your facts are accurate, Ron," he said.

And yet in my interaction with Marquardt, he never denied the facts that I presented in my testimony; he just did not want them presented to the congressional committee. Marquardt wanted me to fall in line with Daren Green as well as the chiefs of police of Ogden and Layton, all of whom submitted written testimony in support of the Clearfield Job Corps despite its negative influence. If I had capitulated to his not-so-subtle demand to suppress the truth in my testimony, it would have been akin to accepting a bribe.

But my integrity was and remains inviolable. I had negotiated heroin and cocaine transactions with armed criminals, faced down a seventeen-year-old prostitute hell-bent on killing me while operating undercover, and run into a raging apartment building fire to rescue an incapacitated mother and carry her down a flight of stairs. Political assaults and threats by the likes of Bob Marquardt did not intimidate me. *I could not then and cannot now be bribed.*

Those 1995 Senate hearings uncovered some damning information. Amid the letters of support for the program was testimony after testimony from around the country that corroborated my experience with the Clearfield Job Corps. They reported, for example, the amount and severity of crime that occurred at Job Corps sites including drug use, beatings, rapes, and even murder. Trainees described "blanket parties" where newcomers were hazed by having blankets thrown over them while they slept and then beaten by as many as ten kids whom they could not identify. The Department of Labor itself cited in a 1994 report that twenty-five Job Corps sites had "histories of excessive" violence. A former gang member from the Bronx turned pediatric dentist eagerly agreed to provide services for his local Job Corps only to conclude that the program was a "ghetto dumping ground" where the priority was to "keep the numbers up so that government checks kept coming in." In 1995 Vermont senator Jim Jeffords launched a campaign to inundate the Labor Department with written requests for data that proved the Job Corps participants were less likely to be incarcerated. Based on its nebulous goals, overreliance on private contractors who submitted dubious statistics, and unchecked misconduct, in her 2003 book *The Failed Century of the Child* historian Judith Sealander roughly estimated that the program cost Americans over $40 billion from 1969 to 1994 and concluded, "The huge sums poured into the Job Corps were wasted."

I had done nothing wrong when I exposed the Clearfield Job Corps, and we all knew it. But making the decision to stand up for what I believed was in the best interest of my job had repercussions. Because of my outspokenness, I was not in a higher position when I retired, but rank and title did not matter to me. What mattered was that I had done the right thing.

And what mattered to my immediate superiors was trying to stop me.

CHAPTER 22:

YOU DON'T HAVE TO AGREE...

The first time Dick Greenwood came to my office, just looking at him made my insides churn with a mixture of contempt, disgust, anger, and hatred. The last time I felt such an avalanche of negative emotions was twenty years earlier after my Black Klansman investigation, when my supervisors Lilly and Dalton had interfered with my career aspirations. Those emotions made me determined to overcome their intrusion, which ultimately led to my relocation to Utah. Now that I had created a thriving career for myself, I found myself in the same position with an equally intrusive yet less competent supervisor.

Despite the obstacles I faced in my position as the state's gang intelligence coordinator, I enjoyed my work. I viewed challenging those who did not want to take the actions necessary to stem the tide of gangs in the state as part of the mission I accepted when I came to Utah. Whether at national gang summits or congressional hearings, the ability to share my expertise at the national level contributed to my sense of duty and fulfillment. And I always had the support of Commissioner of Public Safety Doug Bodrero, who had created the position for me.

Then Bodrero retired in 1996, and with his departure, the proactive approach I had long advocated for dealing with the gang problem was jettisoned. When he was promoted to the commissioner of the Department of Public Safety, the governor had asked him to provide names of candidates to replace him as deputy commissioner. Bodrero did so but his list did not include Lieutenant Richard "Dick" Greenwood, who at the time was the head of the governor's security detail. The governor reportedly told Bodrero to revise his list by adding Greenwood's name to it.

When former sheriff of Weber County in Ogden Craig Dearden succeeded Doug Bodrero as the commissioner of public safety, those departmental politics kicked in. Dearden immediately proved to be out of his element and fell under the sway of Deputy Commissioner Dick Greenwood. Seeking to upend the norms of DPS operations, Greenwood would become my archenemy in my fight against gang violence. The antics of Joe Ritchie, Aleck Shilaos, or anyone else in the community would pale in comparison with the lengths to which he went to prevent me from doing my job. He personified the word *incompetent.*

Remember that when the Utah Narcotics and Liquor Law Enforcement Bureau recruited me, they assured me that my role would be independent of the highway patrol. For officers who had devoted our careers to being undercover narcotics agents, wearing a uniform or otherwise being required to do any of the mundane work expected of a highway patrolman was a non-starter. We had fulfilled our stint in uniform including working as traffic enforcers so expecting us to return felt like putting our careers on a backward spiral. In my case, putting me in Utah Highway Patrol uniform after nearly twenty years of undercover work would be not only unfulfilling but also insulting.

But Dick Greenwood was hell-bent on designating all sworn personnel as Utah Highway Patrolmen and making them wear the uniform associated with monitoring traffic on the state's highways including undercover agents. Although I was a gang investigator, I was technically assigned as a narcotics investigator so his ridiculous mandate also applied to me. Although narcotics cops and highway patrolmen both fell under the purview of the Department of Public Safety, we had a distinct group of supervisors independent of traffic monitoring functions. But Greenwood was a career highway patrolman, and it became clear that his intention was to remove all the agents in high-profile positions in narcotics, liquor enforcement, special investigations, and intelligence and replace us with personnel whose experience with law enforcement was limited to traffic violations. They promoted traffic cops to lieutenants and raised their pay as well as increasing the pay of sergeants in the highway patrol so their salaries equaled those of narcotics cops. Furthermore, they forced other sergeants like me to report to the highway patrol lieutenants. By placing narcotics cops under the supervision of lieutenants who were career traffic cops, they ensured that we could not get the advice or approval required to do our jobs, because our supervisors had no knowledge of police work beyond monitoring the state's highways. In addition, they arrogantly refused to acknowledge their lack of narcotics experience, which furthered the rift between us.

Dearden and Greenwood's ill-conceived agenda also failed to consider how the vast trove of knowledge that we possessed would be lost forever. There is a learning curve to undercover investigations, and at that time *no* traffic cops in the Utah DPS met the threshold of experience required to perform such specialized police work, much less supervise those assigned to it. Yet they assigned a trooper—the late Captain Dennis Wendel—to head the state narcotics bureau. Meanwhile, Wendel knew nothing about narcotics investigations and viewed that world through the lens of a traffic cop.

Wendel immediately revoked $500 in state funds advanced to narcotics cops to conduct undercover drug buys and related expenses even though our agents dutifully submitted to audits on average twice every year. He maintained that by using the money this way, we were violating criminal law and state rules prohibiting the possession and sale of illicit narcotics. According to Wendel's reasoning, which Dearden and Greenwood supported, every narcotics investigator operating undercover was breaking the law they were charged with enforcing and subject to arrest. This allegation implied that by buying drugs to enforce Utah state laws, we could be accused of being dirty cops.

Dearden and Greenwood believed that narcotics cops were

unworthy of being called "troopers" and were determined to commit administrative genocide against anyone who had not done "road time." I personally would have rather been called a "nigger" than a "trooper," and I would never tolerate anyone degrading me with that racial slur. Dearden and Greenwood's bias toward non-troopers in the sworn ranks fomented an us-versus-them mentality among those in uniform. They fed this attitude when they replaced those like me with specialized knowledge with career traffic cops like Captain Wendel, and that understandably did not sit well with us.

So the first time I met with Dick Greenwood on one of his statewide tours to meet with DPS sergeants to hear their feedback and concerns, my revulsion was so great, I had to actively restrain myself from spitting in his face. To do so would have been a waste of good saliva. Instead in what some would call an unwise move, I threw down the gauntlet on the deputy commissioner as he loomed in my doorway.

"I am *not* a traffic cop, and I have *no* desire to ever be a traffic cop," I spat. "I did 'road time' with the Colorado Springs Police Department twenty-one years ago, and I do not plan on going back to it." I made it clear to Greenwood: I did not like working in the uniform ranks, had devoted my career toward specialized investigations, and would put up a rigorous public and legal fight against them if Dearden or he attempted to put me in a Utah Highway Patrol uniform.

"You made the career choice to be a traffic cop," I said. Greenwood did not respond, but I could tell by his facial expression that my objection had registered. Because of my defiance, Dearden and Greenwood decided that I was not a team player.

Another responsibility I had as the state's gang intelligence coordinator was to write biennial reports on the status of gangs and law enforcement's response to them. To complete these reports in 1993 and 1995, I traveled throughout the state to interview police officials, join them on ride-alongs to observe their experiences firsthand, and conduct trainings. Soon after that first meeting with Dick Greenwood, I began working on the 1997 report. But when I announced my tour of the state, my lieutenant told me, "The captain has been told by the commissioner's office that you're not allowed to make this trip."

"Then how am I supposed to write this report?" I asked. "How am I supposed to do my job?"

"Go ahead and do the report, Ron," my lieutenant said. "By phone only." But I refused to write the report under that condition, and no one has produced a biennial report on gangs since.

I insisted on sharing my knowledge by any means available to me, and in June 1997 I received another invitation to testify before Congress. The US House of Representatives Judiciary Committee's Subcommittee on Crime held a hearing focused on gang-related witness intimidation and retaliation. The legislators were specifically interested in law enforcement's increasing inability to successfully investigate and prosecute criminal cases because key witnesses refused to testify out of fear of retaliation by gangs across state lines. While I intended to address that particular topic, I was determined to seize the opportunity to impress upon them the need to understand gang culture and its appeal to young people and the imperative of listening to gangsta rap music as the way to do both.

As I predicted, Linda Sue Davidson initially won her case against Time Warner, only for the company to appeal and the federal court to rule against her on March 28, 1997. It dismissed the cases against *Soldier of Fortune* as viable precedents, determining that the likelihood a listener of *2Pacalypse Now* would act upon Tupac's messages was substantially less than a person responding to a magazine advertisement seeking to hire a "hit man." In the case against the magazine, the plaintiff presented evidence that connected at least seven classified ads to criminal activity, whereas Davidson failed to link Tupac's album to any other claims of incitement despite selling more than four hundred thousand copies. As to whether Time Warner should have reasonably foreseen that distributing *2Pacalypse Now* would lead to violence, the court countered that Trooper Davidson's killing was an attempt by a gang member to evade justice for driving a stolen vehicle and not a random act of violence. "To be sure, Shakur's music is violent and socially offensive. This fact, by itself, does not make violence a foreseeable result of listening to '2Pacalypse Now.'" Finally, the court ruled that the album could not be excluded from First Amendment protection on the grounds of obscenity. While filled with expletives and violence—"overall, the album is extremely repulsive"— it did not satisfy the Miller test that the Supreme Court uses to determine whether speech or expression is obscene and, therefore, not protected by the First Amendment. *2Pacalypse Now* lacked the patently offensive representations or descriptions of masturbation, excretory functions, and lewd exhibition of the genitals required to be deemed obscene.

Ultimately, the court disagreed with the plaintiff that the lyrics of *2Pacalypse Now* imminently incited Ronald Ray Howard's violence toward Trooper Davidson. "No rational person would or could believe otherwise nor would they mistake musical lyrical poetry for literal commands or directives to immediate action." It also expressed a wider societal concern that any ruling in favor of the Davidson lawsuit would result in self-censorship by broadcasters, recording artists, and the like, who would in essence be forced to concern themselves with the potential for liability their words could have on people beyond their control. They felt such self-censorship would "also prevent listeners from accessing important social commentary, not just the violent and aesthetically questionable *2Pacalypse Now*. The public, like Mr. Shakur, has the right to access 'social, aesthetic, moral, and other ideas and experiences.'"

"'2Pacalypse Now' is both disgusting and offensive. That the album has sold hundreds of thousands of copies is an indication of society's aesthetic and moral decay," said presiding judge John D. Rainey. "However, the First Amendment became part of the Constitution because the Crown sought to suppress the Framers' own rebellious sometimes violent views. Thus, although the Court cannot recommend '2Pacalypse Now' to anyone, it will not strip Shakur's free speech rights based on the evidence presented by the Davidsons."

So imagine the Congress members' surprise when several months later at the gang retaliation hearing, I sat before them and broke out in rhyme seconds after my introduction.

Raised in the system, gang affiliate,
Amerikka, take a look at what you created
It started in the section, grew like an erection
spread like cancer, now the country's infected.

"Those words, gentlemen, are lyrics to a rap song titled 'Gang Bangin'.' They clearly illustrate the nature and complexity of any issue dealing with the subject of criminal street gangs," I said. Then like a translator, I interpreted every line I had just spat and its implications for the epidemic growth of street gangs in the United States. "American society is truly engaged in a civil war where this problem is concerned. It is a war, I am sad to say, we as a nation are losing."

By the time I finished testifying, I had performed bars from ten rap songs, some almost in their entirety and none censored. While I was known for my ability to decipher gangster rap and correlate its lyrics to street crime, the scope of my testimony that day encompassed far more than the narrow topic of witness intimidation. After twenty-three years of experience on the front lines and countless hours of independent study, I felt compelled to seize this opportunity to raise the broader issues in criminal justice and used the rappers' words to punctuate my perspective on how we were failing and what we should be doing instead. Becoming a "hip-hop cop" meant that many of the positions I had taken three decades ago not only put me in direct opposition to most in the law enforcement community but also aligned me with some of today's demands for criminal justice reform.

For example, when this hearing took place, the "super-predator" theory had gained major traction. Today we recognize how that racist term effectively pathologized Black youth, depicting them as soulless marauders, terrorizing the streets of America and disproportionately committing rape, murder, and other violent crimes—an apocalyptic prediction the statistics never substantiated. Not then, not now. But in the mid-1990s, the media's prolific yet uncontested use of the term fueled hysteria, and in response legislative bodies across the nation were rushing to reclassify juvenile offenders as adults, some as young as fourteen. In my congressional testimony, I railed against this adultification as unnecessary and ineffective, in part because it was based on sensationalism. "Studies have shown, however, that juveniles account for approximately 10 percent of all violent crime in the country," I said. "A figure that, according to a report by the National Council of Juvenile and Family Court Judges, has not changed in approximately 30 years."

I also shot at tough-on-crime measures including then president Clinton's Violent Crime Control and Law Enforcement Act, better known as the 1994 Crime Bill, which was hailed by the law enforcement community. Remaining the largest crime bill in the nation's history to this day, the bill, among other things, allocated $9.7 billion for prisons, and I minced no words about my disdain for such an exorbitant investment in punishment over prevention. "Perhaps the most egregious example of the legislative response to the rise in crime is the belief that putting more people in jail/prison will ease the public's pain of victimization," I testified. "The influx of business has resulted in the privatization of the penal institution, making it one of the most profitable business ventures in the country. It has made fortunes for those businessmen who wallow in the misery of others. Unfortunately for the inner-city minority, they, too often, represent that 'other.' Legislative 'get tough' measures all too often go hand in hand (or is it hand in pocket) with the privatization of the penal colonies in this country."

I cited federal sentencing guidelines for crack cocaine versus the powder variety as another example of socioeconomic disparity. "The sentencing discrepancy is frequently applied in rap lyrics to show that in spite of its claims to being a fair and just society, the American judicial system is heavily weighted in favor of those with the 'money and power' (to quote from a song by the same name)," I said. "It is a system, they say, that prefers to focus on the powerless inner-city minority crack fiend who is on the back end of the cocaine express food chain, instead of the powerful white importer who controls the switch that sets that engine in motion. Cocaine is cocaine and the basic laws of math still dictate that 500 grams is greater than 5 grams."

And showing zero tolerance for zero tolerance, I argued that "get tough" measures were failing to impede crime among youthful offenders and only served those financially invested in the prison industrial complex. Taxpayer dollars were better spent on viable alternatives, because the cost of incarceration and rehabilitation efforts far exceeded the cost of prevention. Yet I had to recognize the resistance to this approach in my testimony as well. "Unfortunately supporting this agenda represents the ideological antithesis of the privatized prison industry. In the political climate of today it is not in the best interest of elected officials to advocate prevention and intervention efforts over the building of more prisons for human warehousing," I said. "To do so would be a political death knell."

In my takedown of the zero tolerance philosophy with which law enforcement, prison profiteers, and elected officials were so enamored, I called out its flaws as a policing strategy.

As a strict enforcement of the letter of the law, zero tolerance demands the arrest of an individual involved in gangs for any offense no matter how insignificant including things such as the possession of tobacco by a minor or drinking beer in public. This robs investigators of the ability to assess situations and make an informed decision in the best interest of the community—for example, choosing to escort a first-time offender home instead of taking him to the juvenile facility, speaking with his parents, and otherwise opting for measures that build trust between the police and the people they serve, as Kevin and I had with every onetime pass. You may argue that zero tolerance is a viable response when the community is frightened, but as I testified, such fear results often from over-sensationalized media coverage of high-profile criminal events and the rhetorical hype they inspire. It then leads to high arrest statistics, which I already described as insignificant in accurately evaluating efforts in reducing the juvenile/

gang crime rate. Then those meaningless statistics are publicly touted as evidence of law enforcement's effectiveness in its "war" against gangs in an effort to appease the frightened public.

The positions I espoused in my 1997 statement before Congress were unusual for any member of law enforcement, never mind during that time, and I said as much. "In the politically charged partisan climate of 1990s America, advocating anything less than the total enforcement of the letter of the law is enough to incite heated invective from those entrenched in the philosophy of zero tolerance. Failure to toe the zero tolerance line is seen as a 'break' in the ranks of the 'thin blue line,'" I said. "Advocating any alternative other than that preached by law enforcement administrators as 'divine mantra' is seen as 'selling out' the brethren in blue, of being a 'social worker' instead of a cop."

I concluded my testimony by calling out the failure to scrutinize the music listened to by domestic terrorist Timothy McVeigh who two years earlier had bombed a federal building in Oklahoma City that killed 168 people, including 19 children, and injured 680 others. I redirected their censure from gangsta rappers to the white record executives who gave money and fame to inner-city minority youth for venting their valid frustrations with their social conditions. "Condemn the industry moguls, gentlemen, but listen to the words of their protégés," I advised, "because in them the nature of this 'civil war' can be understood and hopefully addressed in a way that is beneficial to all Americans."

I asked the committee members to "follow rap music as a means of maintaining the social pulse of America, especially as it beats in the heart of the inner cities. That pulse is in a rapid state of flux brought on by an agitated sense of rage and frustration...The youth of America, especially those living in the inner cities, are hurting physically, but more importantly, emotionally. They feel a sense of loss and abandonment by a system they feel does not care about them or their needs. They have become jaded by the strain of growing up in a state of depression, violence and neglect. They are frightened, frustrated and angry but have a difficult time finding a voice to put a name to their feelings of despair. Rap music, especially gangster rap, has given them that voice and allowed them to name that which is causing their pain...Let us try to understand the root cause of their pain in the form of their lyrics. Let us not be controlled by negative emotion but rather seek to find common ground to try to alleviate the cause of their anguish."

The US House of Representatives invited me to speak about gang retaliation and witness intimidation, and I did address that topic, but I also took a stand against the dehumanization and criminalization of Black youth, outlined an agenda for criminal justice reform that had repercussions beyond the issue of gang violence, and not only opposed the censorship of gangsta rap music, but urged my audience to heed the lyrics. Throughout my testimony, I would repeat a bar of my own. "You need not agree with it, you simply need to understand it!"

Unfortunately, too many in Utah refused to listen, never mind understand. The respect I was commanding throughout the country remained elusive from some quarters back in the Beehive, and I could foresee my clash with Dick Greenwood coming to a head. Recognizing that the new administration and I were on a collision course, I joined the Utah Highway Patrol Association for the sole purpose of having access to their legal support in the event of a potential court battle. The irony is that I would clash with another organization that based on its mission should have supported me when I did take on DPS.

CHAPTER 23:

STRAIGHT EDGERS AND RACE BAITERS

While gangs often form along racial lines, their objectives and activities are rarely racially motivated. This holds true for even their most violent crimes, which are usually the simple result of male bravado run amok. Failure to recognize and address that dynamic and instead attribute the destructive behavior of gang members to racial pride or self-preservation is a fool's errand that allows them to escape accountability for the harm they cause communities, starting with their own cultural group.

Unfortunately, we had some influential fools in Utah.

State Street is a popular cruising spot for local youth in Salt Lake City, and Halloween 1998 began as a typical Saturday night. On the sidewalk at the intersection of South and State Streets stood members of a gang that called themselves Straight Edge. This is an unusual gang that could only emerge in a conservative environment like Utah. Mostly white and middle-class, members sport tattoos and piercings, frequent the punk-rock scene, and promote clean living. They do not drink, smoke, or take drugs. Straight Edgers preach against sex outside of marriage, champion animal rights, and are militant vegetarians.

And like any other gang in Utah, Straight Edgers are violent.

For kids who present themselves as clean and claim that violence contradicts their philosophy of living, they were on our radar for vandalism, fighting, and even firebombing. Sometimes their targets were fast-food stands and clothing stores that sold leather and furs. But they were also known to brutally discipline their own members who failed to adhere to their strict lifestyle.

That Halloween night just before midnight, two carloads of teenagers stopped at the intersection for a red light. The teens were Black and Hispanic, allegedly members or affiliates of the same gang. Which group began the taunting—the kids in the cars or the Straight Edgers? It depends on who you ask. One fact remains indisputable across all accounts: Racial epithets were hurled, and violence erupted.

Jaynell Latay Cooper, Black, nineteen, and some of his friends jumped out their car to fight the Straight Edgers. Fifteen-year-old Bernardo Alfonso Repreza and several of his friends rushed from the other car to join the melee. The unfolding altercation had drawn over one hundred onlookers when it turned deadly.

The Straight Edgers beat Cooper over the head and stabbed him in the thigh. Repreza attempted to jump back into his car, but his girlfriend, who had been driving, was stalled at the scene. The Straight Edgers pounced on the vehicle and broke the rear window. When Repreza took off on foot, they gave chase until they ran him down and proceeded to beat him. After Andrew Moench, eighteen, hit him with a bat and knocked him unconscious, Sean Parley Darger, seventeen, struck him again with a "spring billy"—a spring-loaded baton. While Repreza was down, Colin Reesor, seventeen, stabbed him once in the abdomen. As they fled the scene, Reesor told his friends, "I can't believe I stabbed that guy."

The paramedics found Repreza and rushed him to the hospital. The Straight Edgers had broken his nose and fractured his skull, but the teen ultimately died from the four-and-a-half-inch knife wound that severed his aorta. When police arrived at the scene, they found screwdrivers, knives, and clubs. Reesor blindsided his parents when he confessed to his involvement in the fatal brawl over Sunday dinner after church services. Days later Moench, Darger, and he were charged with first-degree murder, but the crime reverberated in the community for weeks. The Repreza family had to locate his brother—a marine serving overseas—before they could bury him in Los Angeles.

Despite the racial exchange that culminated in violence, we ultimately concluded that the murder of Bernardo Alfonso Repreza that Halloween night was gang-related and not racially motivated. In addition to the involvement of Straight Edge, Cooper himself was a gang member with an arrest history. Repreza's friends insisted that even though he liked to hang out with gangs, he himself was not a gang member, but my experience has proven repeatedly that there is no such thing as wannabe.

The local NAACP, however, wasted no time in exploiting the situation to capitalize on Utah's history of racial paranoia. In March 1965, three hundred members of the local NAACP demonstrated in front of the Church Administration Building to compel the Mormons to support pending civil rights legislation. That August a riot broke out in Watts, Los Angeles, and caused unrest around the country for six days, including in Northern Utah. With its annual general conference only a couple of months away in October, the Mormon Church feared that the NAACP would target the event to elevate racial tensions and incite riots. Among numerous lies, rumors alleged that the NAACP was importing "transient Negros" and "Berkeley agitators" into downtown Salt Lake City and stockpiling weapons, allegedly including seventeen missing bombs from Hill Air Force Base in Davis County. It was also said that the NAACP sponsored the arrival of two thousand "professional demonstrators and Black Muslims." The *Daily Utah Chronicle* lambasted the news citing "the evil nature of the rumors" and castigated local leaders for engaging in "backyard speculation." The LDS general conference came and went without incident, and when the local NAACP conducted its own investigation into the rumors, it alleged that they were spread by "certain right-wing societies that make a practice of scaring people"; from there, it added, "some people in the police department and Utah National Guard have continued to help spread the rumor."

This time not only was the false racialized narrative fueled by the NAACP, it contradicted our investigation into the killing of Alfonso Repreza. With the prodding of the president of the Salt Lake City chapter of the NAACP Jeanetta Williams, the parents of a Black gang member involved in the tragedy contacted a news reporter whose coverage created a media frenzy. The story became not about gang violence but about a supposed race war in the city. "It could be that they don't want Utah to be thought of as a place where there are racial problems," Williams told the *Salt Lake Tribune* about a week after the stabbing. "Everybody has gang problems. So what?" she continued. "But if it's a race problem, well, they just don't want that, to have it labeled like that."

Her insistence on this angle both infuriated and concerned me. Not only did her comments trivialize the severity of our gang problem, but we had not uncovered any evidence that Repreza's killing was motivated by race. Williams's narrative threatened to hinder not only our investigation but also our efforts to keep the public calm and informed. To achieve our overall mission to reduce gangs, we had to educate people about why they existed and how they operated, especially when they were struggling to understand how a terrible crime like this could occur and how we could prevent such tragedies in the future. The answer was not to terrify them into bracing for an imaginary race war. The hostility that culminated in a young man's violent death on Halloween night could spread and escalate beyond State Street. Police had already responded to several fights at Repreza's high school in the aftermath of his killing.

We needed the NAACP as an ally not an obstacle. Despite my skepticism toward the organization based on the questionable ways leadership had handled media in the past, I asked to meet Williams at her office to educate her on the dynamic of retaliation that drove gang conflict. She agreed, but I went into that meeting doubtful that she would heed my concerns and tone down her inflammatory rhetoric. Nevertheless, I could not allow my cynicism to prevent me from trying. The NAACP wielded considerable influence in the community, and I had to do all I could to convince her to cease perpetuating an untruthful and even dangerous narrative.

It was my job to nip that "race war" story in the bud.

"Contrary to what you're telling the news media, gang violence doesn't revolve around skin color," I said. "The issue of respect is the source of much conflict between gangs, and when a member perceives a slight to his gang, reputation, or ego by someone in another gang, he feels the need to retaliate. The clash over colors is not Black versus white versus brown or anything like that. It's about Bloods red versus Crips blue versus Varrio Loco Town green."

Despite my attempts to educate Jeanetta Williams, she continued to take to the media to rail against this alleged hate crime against an "innocent Black child." I cannot say that it was a result of my meeting with her, but at least she stopped characterizing our gang problem as an irrelevant nuance. "Whether it is gang-related or racially motivated, we all need to do something," she said to the *Deseret News*. "This violence is intolerable."

Still, the ensuing coverage fed the public belief that the city was embroiled in a racial conflict instead of a gang problem, and claims of a possible Black-versus-white race war dominated the media. The gang unit fielded inquiries from reporters about this nonexistent conflict for days, and my white colleagues referred them all to me. Every time Kevin and I held public forums, we were bombarded with questions about "hate crimes" and the probability of a race war in Utah. Whenever a news outlet ran with that false racial narrative, I would contact the reporter and try to tamp down the paranoia with facts, but I can only recall one reporter who took my efforts to heart and questioned the NAACP's angle. Frustrated and angered by this time-consuming and dangerous distraction, I did not hold back, calling out the NAACP for race baiting as well as the media itself for running with that angle before the Salt Lake Area Gang Project could investigate the Straight Edge homicide and report its findings. It took two weeks—a lifetime in the media news cycle—for the public frenzy to dissipate. While Darger eventually would be acquitted, Moench and Reesor were convicted, sentenced, and incarcerated for the murder of Repreza.

The local NAACP was not the only obstacle to the gang unit's effort to maintain positive relationships with the public. Some activists sought to sow and exploit the understandable distrust that racial minorities harbored against law enforcement for their own aggrandizement. Although the Hispanic-Latino community represented only 6 percent of the total population in Salt Lake City, their youth made up approximately 50 percent of gang members. Carlos Jimenez, the director of human rights at Salt Lake Community College, was a media hound, eager to present himself as the defender of the rights of Hispanic-Latino gang youths and make a name for himself by being contentious toward law enforcement. He went so far as to accuse the gang unit of the wholesale profiling of Hispanic kids. "If a Hispanic elementary school kid flashes a peace sign, they say he's a gang member," he once told the *Salt Lake Tribune.* "If he uses gang lingo, they say he's a gang member...If they even live in a neighborhood where there are known gang members, he's counted as a gang member."

This was not true. Recognizing the harm in stereotyping young people, the Salt Lake Area Gang Project taught parents, teachers, and other concerned adults ways to distinguish gang members from other youth who might wear the same fashions. We used specific criteria for identifying gang members before adding them to our database, and sometimes they were forthcoming and made it easy. Regardless of race, gang members are proud of their affiliations and quick to claim their sets. Finally, Kevin has been designated as our unit's go-to person on all matters related to Hispanic gang members. Being white and unable to speak Spanish, he always felt out of place in this role, but nonetheless Kevin dedicated himself to trying to understand the plight of being a minority in a predominantly white environment. Many Hispanic gang members came to hold "Crane" in high regard because he saw these young men as people and sought to counsel them as best he could. The fact that they sought counsel from a white cop was a testament to Kevin's character.

None of that mattered to Jimenez. As far as he was concerned, every gang cop assumed all Hispanics were gang members. His advocacy for the rights of gang members only applied to Hispanics with no regard for Black, Asian, or Polynesian gang members if they had no connections to their Hispanic counterparts. Jimenez would support and defend any Hispanic gang member at the expense of everyone else in the gang universe, and he specifically accused Kevin and me of marginalizing Hispanic males even if they were not involved with gangs.

Jimenez held a press party at a popular Mexican restaurant in downtown Salt Lake City to announce the release of his new "gang manual," a 180-page manifesto dubbed *Alternatives to Gangs and Drugs*. Kevin and I heard about this public celebration and decided to attend, knowing that Jimenez was up to no good. The event was an elaborate affair brimming with Mexican culture—mariachi music, folkloric dancers, and good food, although Kevin and I paid for our own meal in keeping with department protocols. I saw Jimenez—the manual tucked under his arm—and approached him. "I'd like to see your book."

He was not surprised to see Kevin and me at all. We encountered him all the time and told him to his face he was full of shit. "No. I don't want the information out just yet."

Then Jimenez walked away to start his address to the crowd. I could have attributed his rebuff to his animosity toward me, but my suspicions ran deeper. Why could I not have a copy after he'd gone to such great lengths to draw public attention to this release? Rather than challenge Jimenez, I joined Kevin at a table to have my lunch and bide my time.

Several speakers praised Jimenez's gang manual, and Jimenez read excerpts of it. Kevin and I were determined to stomach his bluster and enjoy our meal. Then his words began to ring a bell. "This all sounds vaguely familiar," I said.

But in the moment, I could not pinpoint why and knew I had to get my hands on that manual. I kept a strategic distance and a close eye on Jimenez, and when he set down the book on a table to speak with a group of reporters, I swiftly picked it up and headed toward the exit. "Kevin, let's get out of here."

We returned to our office where I began to study it, and I soon discovered why Jimenez's words sounded so familiar. Right there on my desk was a booklet published by the California Department of Justice on gangs in California cities and its approaches to addressing them. Jimenez's "manifesto" was organized in the same format as the CDOJ booklet, with specific references to California cities swapped out for Salt Lake City. The wording of both documents was identical.

Jimenez's gang manual was a complete plagiarism, and the man was a fraud.

The next day, I phoned Jimenez. "I read your manual with great interest," I said leaning back in my chair prepared to enjoy every second of cornering this clown. "And I have a proposal that you should seriously consider."

"What?" I already sensed the contrition in his voice. Jimenez knew that I had caught him in his deception.

"You're going to cease making false allegations against Kevin Crane, me, and the gang unit," I said. "Or I will make this document public and point out the plagiarism—which is all of it—and expose you for what you are. A liar."

A long silence. "Agreed," Jimenez said.

"You're a fraud, and I can prove it."

"Well, can I have my manual back?"

"No. It's mine now. Cut the shit."

I still have that manual to this day.

I support the role that civil rights organizations and other racial justice activists play in society but have little tolerance for people who exploit and even sow racial division to justify their existence, and this experience planted my disdain toward the local chapter of the NAACP. That disdain became a contempt—one I hold to this day—several years later when my conflict with my superiors at the Department of Public Safety came to a head, and I turned to the chapter for support. I could not imagine how low Greenwood would stoop, especially when the fight for my career coincided with an extremely painful battle on the home front that I did not see coming.

CHAPTER 24:

BLINDSIDED

won't be back in until later today," I told my lieutenant. "If I make it back to the office at all."

"You've been taking a lot of time off," he said. "It's interfering with your work."

Between the growing tension with my trooper supervisors and the amount of leave I had taken, I knew this conversation was imminent. And under ordinary circumstances, I would not have provided an explanation. I had earned my paid time off, and how I used that time was nobody's business. The problem was that by mid-1999, I was spending increasingly more time away from the job, running out of vacation time yet planning to take off more time no matter what they had to say about it. I was using it for something far more important than traveling out of state to lecture and testify—a deeply personal reason that I did not want to share with these men whom I neither cared for nor trusted unless I had no choice.

Micki had gone to the hospital for a routine checkup when her physician found something in her esophagus. He conducted several tests and identified the presence of a cancerous tumor.

Her medical team warned that although they could remove it, they could not guarantee that surgery would be sufficient treatment. They removed the tumor, thinking they had gotten it all.

Over the next few months, however, Micki continued to feel ill, so they ran the tests again. The cancer had metastasized from her esophagus to her liver. With the tumor located on its edge, and the liver being the only organ in the body with the capacity to regenerate itself, they could excise the tumor from Micki's liver. However, her doctor explained that this metastasis meant that her cancer had reached stage IV and was terminal.

"I've been taking off so much time because I have to take my wife to the doctors," I said. "She has cancer." I accompanied Micki to every one of her appointments, and when she was receiving treatment, it sometimes required sitting in a hospital all day.

"Oh," said the lieutenant. "Well, it's interfering with your job," he repeated. "You need to look closer at that." And it crossed my mind that he might have been referring to my failure to pass the biannual shooting test.

I have never been a good shot, never claimed to be a good shot, and quite frankly didn't care about being a good shot.

A tremor in my right hand made it difficult for me to shoot straight, and officers had to qualify for their right to carry a gun by passing skill tests, which included a night shoot involving dark or artificial light. Despite the tremors, I had always managed to pass the test, but this year I failed to qualify during the night shoot. Nonetheless, departmental policy allowed officers to take the test a second time, and those who still did not qualify underwent remedial training: sitting in a classroom and reviewing the mechanics of firing a gun as if you were a rookie. After completing this training, an officer would head back to the qualification range for a third time. Upon becoming the commissioner for the Department of Public Safety, Craig Dearden was intent on restricting the number of times an officer could repeat the test before facing termination, but I was not worried about qualifying.

I had much more important things to worry about.

"I will go to my wife's doctors' appointments whenever it's warranted," I said. "If I have to work extra hours to make up the time, I'll do it."

That should have sufficed, but my lieutenant said, "Well, we work nine to five."

Of course you don't work after five, I thought. *You're a damn traffic cop.* While he was still talking, I walked out of his office intent on doing what I had to do: care for my wife and our sons, who were only fourteen and nine when Micki was diagnosed. A subsequent checkup revealed that the cancer had recurred—this time in the center of Micki's liver. In no way could they cut a hole in the middle of the organ and expect it to regenerate. There was nothing else they could do to prolong her life, and she became obsessed with dying and losing her Stallworth boys, as she referred to Brandon, Nico, and me.

I took care of my wife as best as I could, but her transition was painful to watch. I met Micki when I was twenty-two; she was nineteen and preoccupied with her physical appearance. A big-boned woman, she considered herself overweight when she actually was shapely. Still, Micki felt ashamed that her body didn't meet other people's standards and thought she didn't look as good as the other women around her.

"Unless I tell you something's wrong, nothing is wrong with you," I would say, attempting to get her to stop obsessing. "And I've never said it." And I never would.

"I know but…" she would say.

"There is no *but*."

Still, Micki went her entire life very conscious of her body image even as everyone else saw a stylishly dressed woman who was never without makeup. And now the woman who'd always had a sharp sense of style resorted to wearing sweatsuits and tennis shoes because nothing else fit. I knew that was not the real Micki. Between medical procedures and physical conditions, Micki's career with Zions Bank ended because she missed so many days of work.

Shortly after Micki's diagnosis, Dick Greenwood called me into his office to talk. "I understand you have a situation at home," he said. "How's your wife? Is there anything the department can do to help?"

I thought Greenwood wanted to discuss my latest failure to

qualify on the recent firearms drill. I had done it all—retaken the test, completed the required remedial training, tried a third time—but still failed to pass the night shoot. I still walked into that meeting unconcerned. *They can have my gun*, I thought. So it surprised me that Greenwood had inquired about Micki. "I have it under control as best as I can," I said.

"Because we know how hard this has been for you."

"No, but thank you," I said, genuinely touched. "I appreciate it."

Greenwood said, "Okay, well, as you know, you didn't qualify with your weapon." The alarms in my head went off. "We're going to terminate you as departmental policy allows."

Just like that, Greenwood turned off his sympathy like a switch. Even though I knew that he had called me into his office to discuss the gun issue, I never expected him to attempt to fire me over it. This was the first time in my tenure with the department—in my entire career, in fact—that I'd failed to qualify a shooting test. My colleagues advised me to aim to the left of my target so that when I shot a bullet, it went where it was supposed to go. Not only had I passed the day shoot as I always did, but others who had failed at either drill in the past had kept their jobs. I heard rumors about bosses failing to pass the gun drills—from captains to commissioners—yet the firearm instructors looking away and passing them anyway.

For my termination to be Greenwood's true intention for this conversation yet to start it by asking about my dying wife… the anger started building in me. I suspected he had been waiting for an opportunity to get rid of me ever since Dearden became commissioner, and he did not give a damn about the dubiousness of the reason or the impact of the timing. Greenwood asked if there was anything the department could do for me having already decided to dismiss me not only from a position that gave me great satisfaction but also at a time of great sadness.

And the worst was yet to come: Greenwood already had the termination letter on his desk. "Sign this." He pushed it toward me. As far as he was concerned, this was never up for discussion, and that further upset me.

"Commissioner, after everything I have done for this department..." I had worked for the Utah Department of Public Safety for fourteen years and had earned two Distinguished Service Awards—the highest distinction the department bestows. My file was brimming with letters of commendation from peers across the country. The US Department of Justice's National Youth Gang Center had reported that major gang crimes in Utah were the lowest since 1993. "It doesn't amount to anything? Take my gun," I said. My responsibilities as gang intelligence coordinator did not require a gun, and I did not care if I carried one. I cared about the mission. Despite the obstacles, I had made headway in my role and remained committed to doing the work necessary to combat gangs in Utah.

"No, you have to carry a gun, and if you carry a gun, you have to be able to shoot it," insisted Greenwood. "And if you can't shoot your gun properly, you can't be a police officer. We have to fire you."

No, they did not. Law enforcement in Utah qualify for

retirement after twenty years of service, and I only had six years left to earn my pension. I refused to roll over as they sabotaged my ability to care for my family with the inevitability of being a single father looming over me. "What about the Americans with Disabilities Act? You have to accommodate someone with disabilities, and I have one," I said, referring to the tremors. "Make an accommodation for me so I can reach my twenty years."

But Greenwood kept pushing the letter toward me. "After you sign the letter, we're going to escort you down to the personnel office and find a civilian job for you," he said. "We're going to take care of you."

"A civilian job has a thirty-year retirement plan." As soon as I signed that paper, my termination would be official, and I had no reason to trust Greenwood to look out for me. "Would I have to start over?"

"Well, you can't carry over your time," he said. "You'd have to start over on the civilian track."

"Fuck that!"

"That's the policy."

"I ain't doing that."

"Sign the letter, Stallworth." He continued to parrot the departmental policy.

This time when Greenwood pushed the termination letter toward me, I grabbed it and flipped it in his face. "My lawyer will be in touch," I said in disgust and stormed out.

When I contacted the Utah Highway Patrolman Association for legal representation, their lawyers were familiar with

Greenwood's problems with law enforcement personnel. In fact, another seventeen-year veteran investigator three years shy of her retirement—a Latina woman who specialized in Medicaid fraud—also faced termination because of her failure to pass the shooting drill. Despite Greenwood's insistence that firing us was departmental policy, the *Salt Lake City Tribune* reported that our terminations would be the first in the history of Utah's Department of Public Safety over a "once minor setback that under a new interpretation of policy became a potentially career-ending lapse." And while the *Tribune* stated that the terminations did not seem to have racial overtones, it noted that the other investigator was the only Latina while I was the sole African American of any gender among a DPS staff of 342 certified officers and that community leaders warned that our terminations would harm the department's reputation with the public.

I declined to comment to the media and continued to report to duty. I even carried my gun to send a message to Greenwood. He may have removed me from the role of gang intelligence coordinator, but I continued to receive requests from within the state and around the country to lecture, especially on gangsta rap. Even before he created the position of gang intelligence coordinator for me in 1993, former commissioner Doug Bodrero would receive requests for my services and approve them without making me take personal leave or docking my pay. The organizations that invited me paid for my travel and accommodations and so the requests cost the Department of Public Safety nothing, and from the testimonials

Bodrero received about my lectures, he recognized that I was doing something that no one else in the country was doing and how my participation at these conferences was putting Utah on the gang map. But once Craig Dearden became commissioner, I had to weigh these requests because I could only do them on my own time and at my own expense, as I had my congressional testimony. *You cannot stop me from doing what I think is right.* And that meant continuing to do the job I had taken an oath to do.

Not that they didn't try, preventing me from fulfilling requests for my services from individuals and organizations. An incident that stood out was when I had traveled to Albuquerque, New Mexico, to lecture at New Mexico State University and met some ladies from the Navajo nation. Portions of the tribal lands of the Navajo people cross the New Mexico–Utah border, and they had attended my lecture to request my help. During a break in the event, they approached me to express their concerns about gangs on their reservation. The women told me about a specific incident—a drive-by shooting involving two rival gang members in which one of them had died. One was a Blood, the other a Crip; both were members of the same tribal clan. Determined to prevent more violence and concerned about the gang threat to their customs, the tribal leaders invited me to discuss gang culture with their community so they could process what had occurred and identify solutions. Their request came under my purview as the state's gang intelligence coordinator, but my superiors had prohibited me from traveling to fulfill my responsibilities. "Call the commissioner's office,"

I said, advising them to make a direct appeal to Dearden. "Ask him why I'm unable to render the assistance you're seeking."

Within a week, Commissioner Dearden called me. "Why am I being inundated with calls from the Navajo tribe asking for gang assistance?" he said. "They say you're not being allowed to provide it. I don't appreciate being ambushed like this, Stallworth."

"I did not ambush you," I said. "I simply suggested how they could possibly get the assistance they needed." The Navajo tribe never received the assistance they requested. Had the same request come from church authorities, however, the Department of Public Safety would have gone out of its way to accommodate it.

While my lawyers fought Dearden and Greenwood in court, I solicited the support of various elected and government officials. Two state senators, two members of the state house of representatives and the director of the governor's office of Hispanic affairs came to my aid. In fact, one member of the Utah House of Representatives—also the Republican head of the powerful Judiciary Committee—promised that as long as he was in office, I would maintain my position. Behind the scenes, my previous boss and former commissioner Doug Bodrero also advocated for me. They all agreed that after fourteen years of honorable service including being a recipient of two Distinguished Service Awards—the highest award issued by the department—and a Lifetime Achievement Award from the National Gang Crime Research Center, I did not deserve to be treated that way.

I even appealed to the local NAACP, which was still under Jeanetta Williams's leadership. When I contacted them, they agreed unequivocally that I had a valid complaint against the Department of Public Safety. "We can help you," they told me. "But first you have to give us some money." Meaning that even though they believed that my case warranted a response, they would not advocate for me unless I became a dues-paying member. While I believe the NAACP is a necessary organization, that turned me off on that chapter, and since then I have had no use for them.

But I did not need the NAACP. With the support of my professional colleagues both within and outside the state as well as community members across racial lines, Dearden and Greenwood were forced to back down and did not terminate me. However, they did retaliate by removing me from my position as gang intelligence coordinator, replacing me with a trooper without the title or duties. To add insult to injury, they reassigned me to a desk at the Utah Bureau of Criminal Identification to supervise the concealed firearm permit program.

I'm very private and don't go to people for help unless it's absolutely necessary, but I did not have to ask Kevin. Although we were no longer partners, Kevin and I remained friends, and his wife, Debbie, and he offered to help in any way they could. Because they lived so far away, there wasn't much they could do in the immediate term, but the Cranes were always there for me, asking about Micki and what they could do to help our family. Their support enabled me to remain sane at a time when I was under tremendous pain and pressure—grappling with the impending loss of my wife, remaining strong for my sons as they struggled with their own grief, and dealing with heartless assholes at work.

Micki was a member of the AME Church in Ogden, and they can kiss my ass from now until eternity. Those so-called good church people were aware of my wife's battle with cancer, but only one person ever offered our family any kind of support or assistance. She regularly visited Micki, bringing with her delicious home-baked bread rolls. Except for that woman, that church can damn itself to hell for all I care.

The support I got came, believe it or not, from the Mormon Church. We had become good friends with Scott Wilde, the Mormon bishop for the area, and twice he organized a food rally to help us out. Each day one of seven families brought a meal to our home so we would not have to cook. We never knew what we were going to eat for dinner until 6:30 p.m., when someone knocked on our door with dinner in hand. After a long day of chemotherapy treatment at the hospital or on the job working to combat crime amid bureaucrats who did not value that work, I welcomed the warm, homemade food brought to our doorstep with a sympathetic smile and words of support.

All our neighbors were Mormons, and they came to see Micki whenever she was capable of a visit. They also offered to run errands for us, whether to go to the store for something we needed or to take my boys someplace they needed to go so they could have a semblance of normalcy in their young lives. The Mormons did this for my family even though we were not members of their faith.

To this day I remain in touch with Scott Wilde, and I will forever be grateful to the Mormons. After years of my experiencing the church leadership as an obstacle to my professional goal of fighting gangs, their members extended much-needed kindness to me toward a personal goal—to survive a battle that I already knew my family and I were going to lose. A kindness denied me by my superiors at the Department of Public Safety despite all the rhetoric of police being a brotherhood.

CHAPTER 25:

ENDINGS FORESEEN
AND UNWANTED

R on, you have to go back to the school," Micki said. We began
having difficult conversations about my future without her.
"No matter what happens, promise me you'll go back and finish your degree."

Despite her diagnosis, Micki was determined to continue
with her life as much as possible and proved to be a great example of what she was asking of me. As supportive as she was of my
career aspirations regardless of where they led us, she created
her own success wherever she followed me. Micki allowed me
the quiet time I needed to research and write presentations and
testimony and tolerated my absences as I traveled the country
to participate in conferences and hearings even as she pursued

her own educational and career goals. When cancer struck, she had worked her way into the role of assistant vice president of Zions Bank, the largest in the state, and was running her own branch in downtown Ogden while also studying for her bachelor's degree in business through the University of Phoenix. Even when she could no longer work, Micki persisted with her education despite the intense medical treatments and their overpowering effects on her body.

At first, I attempted to heed Micki's encouragement and example and returned to college. But soon attending school while caring for her and raising our sons, Brandon and Nico, became too taxing. I dropped out for a year to prioritize caring for them while remaining our family's sole breadwinner. Micki pleaded with me to re-enroll, and only when she had gained enough strength to resume a "normal" routine did I do so. In her final days, as she lay ill in our bed, she chastised me for taking off that year. "Promise me you'll get your degree, Ron."

"I promise."

She had been in a contemplative mood as she accepted her fate. "And I also want you to promise me that you will find a companion," Micki said. "Find someone who will love you and the boys and take care of you all. Don't give up on affection just because I'm gone."

At first I did not respond to her. Then I said, "I'll take it as it comes." I knew in the moment that I did not intend to actively look for someone else. "If it happens, we'll take it from there."

Micki's illness also did not diminish her dedication as a wife and mother. Like many married couples, we had different parenting styles that sometimes complemented each other and at other times clashed. Cancer did not change that, and while I did not want to prevent Micki from being a nurturing mother to our boys, I felt a responsibility as their father to provide the tough love that would teach them about right and wrong and the consequences of their actions. As a young teen at the time of his mother's diagnosis, I worried that Brandon was especially vulnerable. Like most Black parents, I sat my boys down and gave them the Talk. "This system is designed to fail you as a Black child," I said. "And being the son of a Black cop, you need to be careful and watch out for certain traps." Brandon and Nico received the full treatment, which included how they should behave if a cop ever stopped them. "Don't say anything out of line. Don't cuss, don't yell, don't scream. The cop is in control of that situation," I said. "He ultimately makes the decision on what he will do to you. You don't want to give him any reason to do the worst." Whether they were out with their peers or came across a cop, I did not want my sons to be another statistic, another pawn of the system like Ronald Ray Howard.

Throughout this challenging period, my thoughts regularly strayed to the tragedy of Ronald Ray Howard and Trooper Davidson. His was the first and only capital homicide case of my career, and I remained curious about the outcome. Trooper Davidson left behind his wife, Linda Sue, along with a daughter and son who were in their late teens when he was killed. Two years after his death, his widow would bury her son after a car accident. I always wondered what became of their family as well as the life of Ronald Ray Howard, especially since my testimony was a factor in his conviction.

Ten years after his conviction, my curiosity about the young man got the better of me. I reached out to Howard's attorneys, and they informed me that anti-death-penalty supporters had created a website through which he communicated with the outside world. If I messaged Ronald through the site, they said, he was sure to reply. I wrote him a message requesting a dialogue about his life, the case, and the influential appeal of gangster rap. In a brief reply he sent in September 2003, Howard expressed concern for his grandmother's health and agreed to correspond with me.

> *Mr. Stallworth, I reach beyond these walls because I actually care. It's like I'm in hell, and I want to reach out and warn young people of the pitfalls that could land them in this same type of hell. Or an early grave. I feel sometimes that the warnings are not enough, that I should have a workable answer to offer them, but the only things I know to tell them is to go to school and make sure they do well there, as that is their foundation in life…Easy to say. But when money is needed now, it's not so easy to do.*

Only a month later, Howard sent me a second letter. *Just to let you know that I am very much interested in talking with you about assisting in your efforts,* he wrote. *I do understand that in assisting in your efforts, I am also pushing that much closer to my own struggle.* I wondered if he was referencing his impending execution. In the third letter I received from Howard in November 2003, he reiterated his willingness to converse with me about any topic under one condition: He first wanted to "build a bridge between the two of us" so I could have a better understanding of who he was.

> ...I want you to understand totally, and in full that I am not the person who you will read about in the newspapers, or in court transcripts. I do not attempt to say that I am innocent, or that I am not deserving of some type of punishment. I only want to express that I am not the person who I was made out to be, nor am I the same young kid who I was all those years ago either...

A decade after his conviction, Howard remained conflicted about his actions on April 11, 1992. On the one hand, he said killing Trooper Davidson was wrong and apologized for taking his life. *I have to be honest and tell you that it took me a whole long time to realize that no matter how you took what happened out on the highway that night so many years ago was wrong.*

On the other hand, even though he was driving a stolen vehicle with a broken taillight when Trooper Davidson pulled him over, Howard still perceived himself as the officer's potential victim and the shooting a result of survival instinct. *I felt justified in my heart and mind I was about to be victimized. So the rules of the jungle kicked into place. Self-preservation... Still to this day I feel that I was pulled over for no reason...*He attempted to reconcile the contradictions in his thinking and take responsibility for his actions. *What I am saying is that even if I was right, or am right, I was wrong...Do you see where it is not just about the idea of being regretful. But in realizing the wronness [sic] of it all.*

Howard shared that he was working with college students who had requested assistance with their research on prison life, death row, and growing up in poverty as well as being a mentor to at-risk youth. He took pride that as someone who dropped out of school in the eighth grade he could still be a positive influence and mentioned that one young man under his "supervision" graduated high school and another enrolled in college. *One juvenile in the program wrote and told me how he wasn't out here trying to kill anyone. That he was just a drug dealer out there trying to stack his paper. I gave him a pearl of wisdom my dad once gave me. Only I took the time to show him how when you carry a pistol, you may not be looking for trouble, but you are hoping some one [sic] steps wrong. So in the truest form, you are indeed looking for trouble...Pointing out the pitfalls that I myself fell [sic] to see because of my tunnel vision, and then some that I knew about but made excuses to do what I wanted to do...*

Cognizant of the execution looming over his head, I asked Howard about his mental state with a mix of curiosity and compassion. How did he maintain a sense of sanity with the ever-present thought of death? While our circumstances were radically different, I had the same challenge, confronting the impending death of my wife of twenty-five years while providing stability and strength for the sake of our sons. In his final letter to me in March 2004, Howard attributed his ability to cope to both reflecting on his ancestors—both in prison and on plantations—and focusing on his loved ones. *The chain gangs, the beatings, horses biting me as a form of punishment and so on. I find myself wondering at how those people took living under their circumstances. In both cases I feel that I couldn't do it. That I wouldn't do it! That I would rebel knowing the price of my rebellion is death...They shared a strong Will to Survive...The first rule of life, Self-Preservation. I feel that will to survive is in all of us. Some of us just haven't ever been forced to tap deep enough into that will. So that is how I believe I cope.* Of his children, family, and friends, Howard wrote, *I live for them...I want them to be proud of me. So I refuse to allow certain parts of my life to dictate the whole of who I am. So I push on.*

In that final letter, Ronald Ray Howard also sent me lengthy thoughts on my request for his views on a variety of topics, from the way ghetto youth perceive death to the effects gangster rap had on him. *When I was a young kid, as young as nine or so, I felt the breeze of a bullet and heard it's [sic] beat on the wind as it passed right over my head...in becoming a part of the streets, you accept that in some way that Death might be lurking 'round the corner. The sad part is, in surviving the streets it is seen in some way as a badge of honor. Something akin to the honor of Vets who boldly proclaim with pride that they had been to wars, and had made it through war zones...*

Of gangster rap music, Howard wrote, *People listen to music they relate to the stories told in country music are stories that groups of people can relate to.* He noted that the stories told via rap music, particularly hard-core gangster rap, actually were true stories of everyday life in the ghetto. *Remember what I said about war zones! So being that there is a certain amount of honor that goes with living that lifestyle, it is glorified, and the Rappers are made out to be hero's [sic] in a sense even though the stories told are often over exaggerated. Show me a Vet who hasn't exaggerated his experiences at war when he tells his old war stories. The same goes for Gangsta Rap.* As for how the genre impacted him personally, Howard said, *I wanted to become 'Hard,' I saw respect that those who was 'hard' got, and I wanted that respect as well. So I got involved in the things that would make me hard as well. I don't think I was ever a bully type of person. I think most people who knew me would tell you that I was more of laid back fun loving type of person who wasn't to be jacked with. I had a desire to have fun, to have people like me, but I wouldn't stand to be mistreated. I had had enough of that with my dad...*Howard ended his final letter to me admitting that answering my questions left him feeling a little drained, but he also wished me well and stated that he hoped to hear from me again soon.

I intended to write to him again, but both personal and professional circumstances took control of my life. One morning Micki got out of bed to go to the bathroom and fell. She called my name, and I ran to her. When I took her to the doctor, he informed us that this time the cancer had metastasized to her right hip. The tumor had impacted a nerve, and if he attempted to operate on Micki and cut the nerve, it would cripple her.

From that point on, she was bedridden. I had to carry Micki or put her in a wheelchair to get her wherever she wanted to go. Because of the chemotherapy and radiation, at times she could not eat or even stand to be near food cooking. After bringing her home after one of those procedures, I would ask Micki if she wanted something to eat. She would say, "Yeah, but don't cook." Instead I'd run out to get a pizza or Subway's or whatever it was she wanted. Micki would take only one or two bites of it and have enough. I did what I had to do to take care of her, and while it was very difficult, I've never regretted it.

While I had some fulfilling career experiences after testifying in Ronald Ray Howard's 1993 trial for the murder of Trooper Bill Davidson, by the time of our correspondence, my daily life was another hell. On the one hand, my journey as an expert on gangster rap music and street gang culture took me to Washington, DC, where I testified in three congressional hearings. I also served as a consultant for the Rhode Island Department of Children, Youth and Families at the request of the governor as well as for law enforcement agencies including the Los Angeles Police Department, the Los Angeles County Sheriff's Department, the Bureau of Alcohol, Tobacco, Firearms and Explosives, and even the Drug Enforcement Administration. I taught at the FBI Academy and authored several articles for law enforcement magazines. But despite all these accomplishments that reflected positively on Utah's Department of Public Safety, Dearden and Greenwood were intent on punishing me for challenging their attempts to terminate me six years before I qualified for a state pension while my wife was dying.

I accepted the reassignment to oversee the concealed firearm permit program at the Bureau of Criminal Identification, which enabled me to keep my gun and badge as well as maintain the time I already had earned toward my pension. But I hated the position, spending my days sitting at a desk surrounded by people who believed the be-all and end-all of policing was wearing that damn traffic cop uniform. I still refused to wear it. When the Olympics came to Salt Lake City in 2002, Dearden and Greenwood forced everyone to get two uniforms and all the accoutrements for the highest visibility. I turned my badge upside down, wore that stupid Smokey Bear hat backward, everything I could do to disgrace the uniform and show my contempt. *Fuck the Utah Highway Patrol!* "If you make me wear a uniform again," I said, "I'll become your worst nightmare."

My own worst nightmare became real on November 17, 2004—my son Brandon's nineteenth birthday. Before lapsing into a coma, Micki asked her nurses to remind me to do something nice for him. That was indicative of who she was as a wife, mother, and person—always thinking of someone else. She lived her final day and died that night thinking of her three Stallworth boys. I found it especially cruel that a woman with so many dreams, so much talent had been given less than fifty years to realize them. Between her fighting spirit and commitment to education, she managed to earn her bachelor's degree, and a month before she died, she earned an A in her first course toward a master's degree. Micki made me proud to the very end.

We buried my first wife on what should have been her fiftieth birthday. And even though we were not Mormons, in honor of the neighbors who came to our assistance in our time of need, I chose to hold Micki's memorial at their church. When tragedy struck our family, the Cranes and members of the Mormon faith showed me that some people do walk their Christian talk.

I returned to school after Micki's death, and things were different from when I'd first enrolled in college in Colorado Springs. Few of my instructors were cops, and once I knew their understanding of policing only came from schooling and not also experience, they lost all credibility for me. Call me arrogant, but you had to prove to me that you were knowledgeable about what I was encountering every day for me to make the effort to do well in your course. During my career I often worked with instructors in police programs throughout the country who were purely academics. After hearing me lecture or reading one of my books or essays, some would be surprised that I myself did not have a degree. I respect education, but I am not easily impressed by nor have ever been intimidated by degrees.

When I enrolled in the criminal justice program at Columbia College in Salt Lake City—an off-campus learning institution of Columbia College in Missouri—almost all my instructors were working cops, some with advanced degrees. In October 2007, I kept my promise to Micki and earned my bachelor's degree in criminal justice administration—almost two years after her passing and thirty-six years after I'd first started college.

On October 6, 2005, the state of Texas executed Ronald Ray Howard. He was already dead when I learned of his execution. While I knew Howard's death was inevitable, I was not aware that a date had been set, and only when I attempted to contact him again did I learn that the deed had been done. Before he was administered the lethal injection, he made a final statement to Trooper Davidson's widow, daughter, and brother: "I hope this helps a little," Howard said. "I don't know how, but I hope it helps." He thanked his family and allies for their love and support. While losing consciousness after receiving the lethal injection, Howard looked to a friend and said, "I'm going home. I'm good. Be strong. I'll be alright." Twelve minutes after the injection, Ronald Ray Howard was pronounced dead at 6:42 p.m. on October 6, 2005. At the time of his death, he was thirty-two years old and had lived on death row for thirteen years.

I had mixed emotions about the execution of Ronald Ray Howard. I felt sorry that his social environment had stacked the deck against him, another young Black man's life wasted. But I was also pissed off that Howard had needlessly killed a cop because he presumed the man to be racist when, by his own account, Trooper Davidson had been nothing but professional when he approached the car. Two lives ended. One family was forever altered by the sudden, violent, and inexcusable murder of their loved one, while the family of the person responsible endured a slow march to their eventual loss. Both families—one white, the other Black—lost a father, son, grandson, brother.

Ronald Ray Howard had no justification for killing Texas state trooper Bill Davidson, and yet he had reason to fear the police. The innate repulsion he felt was the result of racist authority figures and the real limitations placed on the lives of young Black men. Like countless inner-city youth, Howard understood that police corruption upheld the governmental denial of equal opportunity to people like him. Gangster rap did not make him do it, but the shameful timeline of law enforcement and intelligence agency racism toward Black Americans that gave rise to the genre in the 1990s persisted.

Perhaps my understanding of that complex reality, combined with my forced transfer out of the gang unit, is why I took such an interest in Jemijo.

CHAPTER 26:

JEMIJO

I was at my barbershop in downtown Salt Lake when a young man walked in decked out in blue from head to toe. Blue shoes, blue pants, blue shirt, blue jacket, blue cap—I immediately knew he was a Crip. When he started to speak, I caught my barber giving him a warning with just a look. *Watch what you say*, it said.

"Why don't you meet me for lunch tomorrow?" I said to the young man. "That Kentucky Fried Chicken down the block."

"Why you want to talk to me?"

"A free lunch. What do you got to lose?"

Although he asked me a few more times why I wanted to meet with him, the young man eventually agreed to have lunch with me and walked out the door.

The next day I got to the Kentucky Fried Chicken earlier

than we had planned to see who came with the young man, if anyone, and otherwise scope him out. I was sitting in a booth when he arrived. He slowly walked up to the window facing the main street, and I watched him check out everyone sitting in the booths. When he saw me there, I waved him in.

He acknowledged my presence but continued looking inside the restaurant through the window. He finally walked through the door but remained by the entrance, again acknowledging me with a nod while scoping the interior. I knew what he was doing. He was checking to see if there were cops in there ready to pounce on him.

Then he strolled around the lobby, checking out everyone sitting at each table. When he finally made his way over to me and sat down, I said, "Are you satisfied there's nobody here but me?"

"How do you know that's what I was doing?"

"I'm a cop. I know how you guys think. And I would do the same thing." Then I said, "Go order yourself something to eat."

He got himself a three-piece meal, and we started to eat. "Why did you want me to meet you here?"

"Because I wanted to talk to you."

"Why?"

"Because you're a Crip."

"How do you know that?"

"Look at how you're dressed."

"Oh, yeah."

"You're a poster child for the Crips."

He said, "I'm not going to snitch on anybody."

"I'm not asking you to snitch," I assured him. "I'm just trying to find out more about you and your lifestyle and where you come from. I want you to educate me so I can be a better gang cop when dealing with people like you."

"Nobody has ever asked me that before."

"Well, somebody has now."

He and I spoke for a little more than an hour, and I learned a few things about him. He was originally from Los Angeles and confirmed my deduction that he was a Venice Shoreline Crip, as was his brother. Furthermore, his mother was a Crippette, and his father was a drug dealer doing time in a California prison for murder and robbery. Unlike gang members who are drawn to or recruited into the gang lifestyle, he essentially was born a Crip. Although he told me about his life growing up, he didn't give me any juicy info about his gang or their activities. That was fine by me because my intention was to get to know him, not to extract that kind of information.

I finally did get his name when I asked for it.

"Jemijo."

"Is this your real name?"

"Yeah, but they call me Loony."

"Is there a phone number where you could be reached?"

"Nah, I don't do that."

"Okay. I'm Sergeant Stallworth, and here's my number," I said, giving him my pager number. "And we'll get together and talk some more."

Over the next few months, Jemijo and I had a couple more meetings. We talked, and he revealed a little more about himself. "How are you making your money?" I asked him one day.

"Why do you want to know that?"

"I'm just curious," I said with a smile on my face.

"I got a way."

"How much dope are you dealing?"

"Now, why are you accusing me of dealing drugs?"

"Because you are. I know you are. You probably have some drugs on you right now, but you notice I'm not patting you down, checking you out." Then I added, "You're gonna get caught in due time, but I give you one promise: I will not be the one to arrest you. Just don't do any of it around me, and you don't have to worry about that when you are with me."

Over time Jemijo admitted he indeed was selling crack but only enough to get by.

Then one day he said he was trying to find a job. "I want to get out of the dope game."

"Let me see what I can I do," I said.

I contacted the director of parks and recreation of Salt Lake City. "I got this kid that needs help," I said. "He's basically a good kid. Just a little confused in the head."

"And why's that?" the director asked.

"He's a gang member, but he's trying to get out of that life-style and needs a job."

I brought Jemijo to the department and introduced him to the director. The next day they hired him at minimum wage. His job was to mentor younger kids who were contemplating getting into a gang and divert them from that lifestyle.

One day the director called me. "Please come down here." Jemijo was acting crazy and threatening to hit people.

When I get there, Jemijo says, "They won't give me my money!"

"What money?"

"The money they owe me."

Having never held a legitimate job, this kid did not understand the real world of work and how some jobs operate. Jemijo had been working there for two weeks, but they had only paid him for one week because the practice was to withhold the first week's pay. At the end of his appointment, they would pay him for the week owed him. But because Jemijo had never experienced anything like that, he thought they were running a scam on him.

I succeeded in calming him down. "Keep your head on straight," I said. Jemijo even apologized to the director and got his pay. He continued to work for the program for another three months until they did away with it.

Jemijo and I maintained our relationship, and one day he said something profound to me. We'd met at another restaurant, where I bought him lunch. "I got something to say to you. No one has ever talked to me the way you talk to me. No one has ever approached me or tried to explain things to me the way you do." Jemijo paused, his eyes getting teary. "You're not my father, but if I had a father in my life, I would want him to be like you."

His words choked me up. "I appreciate you saying that."

"When I told my mom that I was gonna be talking to you,

she said, 'Be careful, baby. He's a cop. You can't trust him.' And that's why I acted the way I did when I first met you." He took a bite of his sandwich. "I told my mom how you are with me and what you've done for me. That's when she said, 'Maybe he's a good cop. Be careful…but maybe he's okay.'"

He rarely spoke to his dad and told him about me too, and he had received the same warning. *Don't trust him. He's a cop. You can't trust cops at times.* But his dad's advice had also changed. *Well, always keep your guard up…but give him a chance.*

Jemijo and I maintained our relationship until he left town, and many years would pass before I heard from him again. After *BlacKkKlansman* hit movie theaters, he called me. "Sergeant Stallworth! I didn't know this about you," Jemijo said. "Why didn't you tell me?"

"It was no big deal."

"Man, I've been telling everybody that I knew you," he said excitedly. "That I worked with Black Klansman and that you were like a father to me."

"And how are you doing, Jemijo?"

"I'm back in LA, working, preaching, helping people get out of the gang world," he said. "I'm doing good."

"Very good. I'm very proud of you," I said. "Keep it up."

Why I had such an interest in Jemijo when he walked into that barbershop, I can't tell you for sure. There was just something about the kid that struck me and made me want to sit down and talk to him. And for a young man like Jemijo to speak to me was dangerous. He didn't have to snitch on anyone to place himself at risk. Although I had been reassigned to the Bureau of Criminal Identification, my reputation among the gangs remained intact, and talking to a known gang officer could have gotten Jemijo in trouble with his gang. I did not take his willingness to meet with me lightly, and when Jemijo scoped out the restaurant before sitting with me, he was looking for not only undercover officers but also anyone he knew. Had he recognized anyone in that KFC, Jemijo would have walked out without a word to me.

Jemijo reinforced my belief of how important it was to address the emergence of gangs as soon as a community is aware of their presence, as well as addressing the core issues that make gangs attractive to young people. I cannot know for certain that if I had met Jemijo earlier I would have been successful in redirecting him from gang life. But I know without a doubt that what I did helped, and every child deserved that chance. Talking with Jemijo not as a gang member but as a young man—without working a case or having an angle—allowed me to become a better cop. I knew the path that I had been on was the correct one, and I still had the desire to do meaningful work—except those in power at the Utah Department of Public Safety refused to allow me.

About a month after Ronald Ray Howard's execution—and near the first anniversary of Micki's passing—I was sitting at my desk at the Bureau of Criminal Identification when I looked around the room at the uniform troopers that surrounded me. *I don't like you people*, I thought. Feeling like a dinosaur that the comet had missed, I resented all these people who did not know the first thing about investigations unless it began with a speeding vehicle or a vehicular collision. *I don't want to be a part of this anymore.* A few days later, I walked to the main office and put in my retirement papers. With a year left to qualify for my pension, I cut a check to the state of Utah for $13,000—the amount owed for credit for one year—so I could retire with twenty years of service and my duly earned pension that they had tried to deny me.

Yet I remained determined to find another way to speak truth to power even if I did not yet know where and how.

CHAPTER 27:

WHEN ONE DOOR CLOSES...

After thirty-two years in law enforcement—the last twenty with the Utah Department of Public Safety—I retired as a recently widowed father of two teenage boys. While I was no longer a cop on the front lines, my work with gangs continued in other capacities. I occasionally was hired as a consultant or asked to serve in an advisory capacity, and one particular incident was typical of the stonewalling I had to endure as a cop.

After returning from a neighbor's fifth birthday party on July 6, 2008, seven-year-old Maria Menchaca was playing in her front yard in the Glendale neighborhood of Salt Lake City. Then three gang members—Frank Puga Benavidez, twenty; Gabriel Alejandro Alvarez, seventeen; and Mae Goodman Johnson, sixteen—drove by the home. They shouted obscenities aimed at Maria's cousin—allegedly the member of a rival gang—and fired several rounds at the house. One bullet hit and killed the little girl.

Menchaca's murder was one of two fatal drive-by shootings that provoked the mayor of Salt Lake City to call for a gang reduction forum. The forum convened government agencies, elected officials, and community organizations to brainstorm effective ways to reduce gang activity in their city and resulted in the formation of a steering committee. Members advised Mayor Becker that if he wanted this initiative to succeed, he should invite me to join their ranks given my knowledge, history, and reputation.

When I met with the mayor, he asked me to co-chair the committee, and I said I would on four conditions, three involving his aide Michael Stott, who sat on the committee as his representative.

One, I wanted direct access to Becker instead of going through Stott.

Two, I wanted my public statements to remain unfiltered—in other words, no interference from Stott.

Three, I wanted my co-chair and I to run the meetings with no intervention from Stott. My co-chair Leticia Medina was a former gang member and director of Duane Bordeaux's Colors of Success. A longtime and well-regarded advocate for at-risk youth who had been appointed by the governor to head his Office of Hispanic Affairs, she had been collaborating with me on gang reduction since 1990. We did not need to be managed.

Finally, I wanted Leticia and I to have input in choosing

future members of the committee to ensure that people knowledgeable on gang issues were part of the equation.

Mayor Becker agreed to my conditions and formally introduced me as the co-chair of the steering committee of the city's
Gang Reduction Program in a press conference on June 26, 2009.

But once again governmental politics quickly reared its ugly
head, and just as I'd suspected, Michael Stott soon became a
major obstacle. Other committee members, Leticia, and I only
cared about stemming the growth of gang culture in Salt Lake
City, but Stott's primary concern was keeping Mayor Becker's
image pristine. In fact, he balked when Leticia and I strongly
suggested he go into the field and experience firsthand what
gang culture was like. Twice he modified my statements to the
media so that they were favorable to the mayor, directly violat-
ing one of my conditions because I myself had no interest in
promoting the mayor's image. And that was only one example
of Stott's encroachment.

When we expressed our concerns about his aide, Mayor
Becker appeared at the next committee meeting to make it
explicitly clear that Michael Stott was his eyes and ears there.
"When he speaks," said the mayor, "he carries the weight of my
office." This, too, was a violation of our agreement.

I insisted on meeting Mayor Becker, and he stood firm in
his support of Stott. That cemented his intention to control the
steering committee's agenda. Leticia and I had no real authority, and he expected us to be his puppets with Stott pulling the
strings. I could not stomach that and immediately resigned.

My last official involvement with the issue of gangs

occurred in 2011 when Davis County attorney Troy Rawl-
ings hired me as his gang intelligence consultant, essentially
hiring me to duplicate the work I had done in Salt Lake City
twenty-three years earlier. When I came aboard, the county
had twenty-three gangs and seventy-one criminals. Yet thirteen municipal police chiefs and one county sheriff had
Shilaos Syndrome, and their excuses ran the gamut. The ones
who privately admitted to me they were aware of the gangs in
their midst lied to the media about their existence. They played
word games to trivialize the problem such as downplaying graffiti as due to a "gang presence"—as if vandalism isn't the first
indicator of an emerging problem that usually escalates into
drive-by shootings and murder—or claiming that gang activity
was "transitory" in nature: committed by individuals just passing through a city that had no "natural" gang environment.
Another claimed there were no gangs in his city because it
lacked places where youth congregated such as a shopping mall
and miscategorized gang activity as isolated incidents caused
by outsiders. The most exasperating denial was the police chief
who insisted outlaw motorcycle gangs were not criminal organizations but social clubs. Like the Boy Scouts.

Meanwhile, despite the public denials and private rational-
izations, all these agencies had officers specifically assigned to
focus on gangs. In the final analysis, my report to the Davis
County attorney concluded that "there is a definite street
gang presence in Davis County and if that presence is NOT
addressed in a more forthright, aggressive manner then that
presence will, as it has throughout this state and the country,

become more firmly entrenched until it is an out-of-control problem completely altering our social, political, educational and economic infrastructure." Every day rank-and-file officers encountered gangs on the street, but pointing this out to their administrative leaders meant running headfirst into political walls of resistance.

I had experienced firsthand the sting of crashing into those same walls, and they reflect why in the last decade of the twentieth century gang culture spread across the country like a metastasizing cancer, taking lives and destroying communities. When I first embarked on this journey in 1988, gang cops in Los Angeles County warned me: Stay focused on eliminating the problem and avoid the politics. They advised me that the key to a serious response was to "jump on it" as soon as gang activity reared its head and attack it with every available resource. Unfortunately, too many politicians squandered too many years using the issue to enhance their political brand, and in doing so wasted valuable time, allowing the culture to grow and consume lives.

Another way I hoped to counter such resistance in retirement (and make some play money) was by teaching. When I taught criminal justice courses at two local colleges, I discovered just how badly our secondary school system was failing young people. Some, like my Polynesian students, had language barriers to overcome, but many of my students had graduated from high school unable to read and write. I spent as much time teaching them how to learn as I did teaching the course subject.

"If you're having trouble with this topic," I said, "look it up in the encyclopedia."

"Professor Stallworth...what's an encyclopedia?"

Granted they had cell phones and the internet by this time, but several students appreciated my instructing them to go to the library to use encyclopedias and dictionaries.

I had one student who was vocal about being a DEA agent but never gave his coursework the necessary attention even though the position requires a college degree. A third grader would have written a better paper than what he submitted.

"With work like this, you're not going to be a DEA agent," I said. "If they were to call me right now, I would not recommend you for the job."

"Why?"

"Because you don't know how to write a report."

"I don't need to know how to write a report," he insisted. "I just need to make the case, and somebody else can write it."

"That's not how it works. You write the report about everything you do, and you don't know how to write a report," I said. "Unless you fix that, you're going to fail this class."

He refused to learn how to write a report and failed the class.

Every time I graded papers, I debated with myself. I wanted to be strict about the writing elements because they had to learn how to communicate properly and proofread their work. But I also wondered if I should give them credit for at least attempting an assignment even if the essay made no sense. I chose to give them credit, but the students still challenged me because

I ultimately gave them a C or D, not the A or B they believed they deserved.

In late 2010 I reconnected with some classmates via the internet to plan a high school reunion for the class of 1971. During my senior year of high school, I had tried out for the varsity cheerleading team as a fluke. The principal announced tryouts over the school intercom. Talking a bunch of shit, I told my friend, "I should try out." I had always been an athlete—a football player, sprinter, and long jumper. I could outrun half the guys on the varsity teams and outjump all of them but one. And this was a time when guys really did not join the cheer-leading squad.

"Stallworth, shut the hell up," he said. "You know damn well and good you ain't no cheerleader."

"Watch me."

On the day of tryouts, I performed two cheers in front of the entire student body. I got the most votes and was elected head cheerleader, to become the second male cheerleader in the history of our school system. I had a handful of people give me grief, poking at me, calling me a sissy, and all that. But they didn't say it too loud or too often because everyone knew I was also a karate instructor who could beat their butts in any competition.

So after introducing myself on the reunion planning message board, a classmate wrote me, "Is this Ronnie Stallworth who was a cheerleader?"

"Yup."

"This is Patsy Terrazas."

Although we had not been friends in high school, I did remember Patsy. We would say hello as we passed each other in the hall in between classes. She was a nice Catholic girl from El Paso.

Patsy and I continued to message each other. As sophomores we both had Mr. Elroy Bode as our English teacher, albeit during different periods. Mr. Bode was the teacher who instilled in me that I had a writing talent and encouraged me to use it. Patsy and I agreed that he was among our fondest memories of high school.

She still lived in El Paso, and a few months earlier had lost her second spouse to cancer. Patsy admitted that she had a crush on me in high school but was too afraid to let me know. I had no idea. We immediately moved our conversation from the internet to the telephone, speaking every day sometimes for as long as five hours. Our high school reunion never happened, but a few months after we reconnected, I invited Patsy to join me in Las Vegas, which had become a getaway spot for me. We met at the airport and headed to the Golden Nugget hotel.

And what happens in Vegas stays in Vegas.

Although I returned to Salt Lake City and Patsy to El Paso, we continued a long-distance relationship for several years, continuing to speak on the phone every day, at least twice a day, often for hours at a time. We eventually would marry, and we remain together to this day. When that good Catholic girl from El Paso came into my life, she didn't only fulfill Micki's wish that I know love again. She filled the emptiness that was in my heart.

I continued to teach, and one evening in March 2013, I had come home after class when something told me to start writing. I followed the whim and picked up a legal pad and pen. I wrote a few pages in longhand, transcribed them on the computer, and then tore up the legal pad pages. Nine months later I had written the first draft of *Black Klansman* with the same process I used to write my police reports, official testimonies, and gangsta rap analyses.

Around the summer of 2015, I made a trip to Salt Lake City and reconnected with Kevin and our partner in the original gang unit, Sergeant Mike Fierro. We met at a Mexican restaurant downtown, and after our meal, I gave them each a copy of the original *Black Klansman* manuscript. Kevin had gotten into motorcycle riding, and when we finished eating and talking, he jumped on his motorcycle and drove off. That was the last time we spoke.

About nine months later Mike called to tell me that Kevin had had an aortic aneurysm and was on life support. Before heading back to Salt Lake City, I called his wife, Debbie, to ask if it would be okay for me to go see him in the hospital. Not only had we developed a personal relationship with the Cranes, it turned out that Debbie had gone to high school with Micki. When Micki graduated from Mitchell High School in Colorado Springs, Debbie was a junior, but she recognized Micki because she was popular and involved in many school activities. What a coincidence that I ended up with a partner whose spouse knew my first wife before I had even met her. From the start it felt as if Kevin and I were fated to be a team. I anticipated that Debbie would say yes to my request to see Kevin at the hospital, and I was grateful when she did.

As always, his family was open and kind to me. So kind that the Cranes included me in their decision to let him go and gave me the honor of being present when they took him off life support. As I shared the last moments of his life with his family, I shed tears for my partner, said my goodbyes, and kissed him on the forehead. Later I laughed, thinking that had he been conscious, he would've said *Whoa!* and stopped me. It was a very lovely moment for me but also a major loss to Debbie, his children Josh, Jessica, and Janeal, and the rest of his family. As his daughter said, "He was my hero."

When Kevin Cranc died on March 25, 2016, it was also a major blow to Utah law enforcement and the community at large. Before the creation of our unit, no one was devoted to studying, never mind investigating, gangs. There was no dedicated effort to keep the streets of Utah safe from their infestation until we came together. Throughout our five-year partnership in law enforcement and the last twenty-seven years of his life as my friend, Kevin taught me about the dynamics of his faith. Even as a devout Mormon, he never attempted to convert me to Mormonism or deny the political obstacles the church posed to our mission. He even had a sense of humor about his faith, like calling the green gelatin with slivers of carrots that Debbie served us for dessert after shepherd's pie "Mormon Jell-O." We were the founding members of the state's first gang unit, and at the time of Kevin's death, there were four gang units throughout the state, some of which I got started with him by my side.

To say that we blazed that trail together and changed the face of Utah's law enforcement is no exaggeration.

There is no greater compliment to a law enforcement officer than to be described as "a good cop," and Kevin was one of the good ones—and not just because he fought alongside me in the quest to squelch the spread of gang violence in Utah. The Hispanic community was upset when the police department removed Kevin from the gang unit. They liked him and wanted him to stay. He understood their kids, who liked him too. Years after his transfer from the gang unit, they asked about him and fondly recalled memories of their encounters with him. They would say they missed Crane, which is astonishing because gang members often don't miss a cop's presence. This was the highest compliment Kevin could have received from the gang members, and he earned it through the tone we set. Gang members don't have to like cops, but if they help us, we will help them. Kevin was a perfect example of someone who did this. A truly good cop. As Mike who had been his patrol sergeant before the three of us became partners in the Salt Lake Area Gang Project noted, Kevin was kind, compassionate, caring, and professional in every way. Just as I quickly came to know firsthand, Mike understood he could count on Kevin no matter the circumstances.

"Kevin Crane was the antithesis of someone who made policemen look bad," he said. "He made policemen look brave, charitable, and kind."

The same year he died, the Metro Gang Unit honored Kevin's contributions and memory by presenting the first

Kevin Crane Commitment to the Community Award at their annual gang conference. Still given every year to an individual or organization who demonstrates excellence in developing, supporting, and strengthening law enforcement and community partnerships, it recognizes Kevin's contributions for forging critical relationships with schools, community agencies, and faith-based organizations to intervene on behalf of young people involved with gangs or at risk of gang involvement. "His effort set a standard for partnerships between law enforcement and community organizations," says the citation. "Those standards include being inclusive, listening to community concerns, and being present in the community impacted by gang activity."

Kevin was the epitome of a great cop and a great friend, and I still think of him fondly and miss him greatly.

CHAPTER 28:

BACK TO BOOTY

At the 2019 Directors Guild Awards, Boots Riley and I eventually crossed paths. Or more accurately, I crossed his. I spotted him across the room and, throwing caution to the wind, got up from the *BlacKkKlansman* table and walked over to him.

I offered Riley my hand. "I'm Ron Stallworth." He was very cordial. Too cordial for someone who a week after *BlacKkKlansman* arrived in US theaters had posted that the film was offensive because its protagonist in the fight against racist oppression was not only a cop but particularly a Black cop. Riley also found that, in the age of Black Lives Matter, the film's premise was incredible and concluded that *BlacKkKlansman* was a "made up story." Worst of all, to bolster his anti-cop views, he accused me of participating in Cointelpro's efforts to destabilize Black radical organizations demanding civil rights. Yet after all the vitriol Riley spewed against me on social media, my name was not registering with him. Continuing to shake his hand, I said, "I'm the Black Klansman."

Booty's smile faded. "Aw, shit!" he said. Then he tried to pull away his hand in disgust.

An avowed communist, he had been a member of the International Committee Against Racism and his father's organization the Progressive Labor Party since he was a teenager. In addition to my police work against the Ku Klux Klan, I chronicled a 1978–79 undercover investigation I did on both groups in Colorado Springs in my memoir *Black Klansman*. During that time, I encountered many Booty Rileys who championed anarchy over constitutional rule. They believed in promoting their nihilistic worldview, the Constitution be damned, while insisting on respect for the letter of the law where their own rights were concerned. I viewed these political agitators as self-serving hypocrites.

But in that moment, I laughed at Riley, gripping his hand tighter. He made another attempt to wrest it away from me, but then I placed my other hand on the back of his neck. By that time, everyone at the *BlacKkKlansman* table realized where I had gone and was freaking out that I was breaking my promise not to publicly confront him. At this point, I had dealt with enough people like Boots Riley to know how to get my message across in the appropriate manner. I maintained a smile on my face to avoid the appearance of conflict while I began to squeeze a pressure point on Riley's neck behind his ear. Unable to wriggle from my grip, Booty reasserted his communist position that I had vilified his father's organization in my book and had worked for Hoover's FBI against Black radical organizations.

"Liar. Prove it," I said, clutching his hand in my left grip while tightening my right hand on a pressure point, sending jolts through his body. In his aggressive critique of *BlacKkKlansman*, he had called me "the villain" who "was part of COINTELPRO. COINTELPRO's objectives [were]...to destroy radical organizations, especially Black radical organizations." Cointelpro was active from 1953 through 1971 when it was exposed after four people broke into the FBI's Pennsylvania office, stole over a thousand classified documents, and mailed them anonymously to several newspapers across the United States. When Hoover headed the FBI in 1971, not only was I in high school in El Paso where there were no Black radical organizations, but I was too young to work for any law enforcement agency in an investigative capacity never mind the FBI. "Produce the Freedom of Information Act documentation you claim exists about me. I dare you!"

Riley did not reply but attempted again to pull away from me while I continued to smile to dispel any notion that we were in an intense conflict. As a proud Black man in AmeriKKKa especially in the age of Trump, I would never submit to another man's hostile attempt to exercise dominance over me. But when I confronted Riley at the Hollywood and Highland Center that night, he was as docile as a lamb, his manhood escaping beneath my grip. His placid response to my exertion of physical control over him demonstrated that he had been punked out by a man eighteen years his senior. To quote the pimps I used to impersonate while undercover, I made Booty my bitch.

While the film adaptation *BlacKkKlansman* was "based on a true story"—meaning it took some liberties with the storyline—the facts of the investigation I conducted largely remained intact. There is no Freedom of Information Act documentation available about my working with the FBI to "sabotage a Black radical organization" because it simply *does not exist.* The only Black organization I had contact with during the investigation was the Colorado College Black Student Union; I had only a single brief encounter with them one night and not over a three-year period as Booty claimed.

His inflammatory and reckless claim was false and points to a double standard, because for a communist-inspired community activist in a predominantly Black community like Oakland where Booty lives, being accused of snitching for the FBI could end his career, and he would never stand for it. And yet this Black man chose to demean another by labeling him a snitch for J. Edgar Hoover's FBI. To paraphrase my late mother, Booty showed his ass; only the worst kind of race traitor would lie about another Black man to promote his self-interest. His tactic was akin to the "house niggas" of slavery who sought favor with white slave masters at the expense of "field niggas."

People like Riley only see me as a cop—the archenemy of Black people. Blinded by their quest to assert their own Blackness, these radically militant individuals cannot accept me in the "collective club of Blackness" that requires everyone else's sense of racial identity to pale in comparison with theirs. Booty would define me solely by my profession and as a traitor to the Black community rather than by our shared experience of being forcibly brought to a hostile land, members of the same group who did not voluntarily come to the shores of America in search of a better life. He reminded me of those gang members, pimps, and drug dealers who challenged my authority to arrest them—even as I was handcuffing them and placing them into the police car—because they were from Los Angeles or New York City. Just as their big-city experiences did not faze me, Booty's radically militant Blackness did not impress me.

Later that night, I ran into Riley again in the men's room as I was exiting the stall. "Aw, shit!" he said again when he saw me then scampered out. When I finished in the bathroom, I stopped by Riley's table on my way to my own. I leaned in close to him, slapped my hand on his shoulder, and said, "I forgot to wash my hands."

CHAPTER 29:

THE CHALLENGE

They might chase me out of the state with a noose, I thought, but I still accepted the invitation with the intent of speaking truth to power.

The first time I delivered a lecture at the annual conference of the Texas Gang Investigators Association was around 1993. I think it might have been the TGIA's third conference or so, and of course they wanted me to speak about gangsta rap. Thirty years later they approached me again based on the success of *BlacKkKlansman.* The organizers asked me to talk about writing the book, my experience with the movie—everybody wants to know what Spike Lee and Jordan Peele are like—and then close with a little bit about gangsta rap.

Although I agreed to cover those topics, I was also determined to speak about things they had not asked me to address.

Shortly after the release of *BlacKkKlansman* in theaters, David Duke went to the trouble of getting my telephone number and called me to express concern about his depiction in the film. Our conversation lasted almost an hour, covering a range of topics beyond his portrayal in *BlacKkKlansman* and including Donald Trump, whom Duke insisted was not a racist. In the current political climate, I felt it important that in my lecture to the over nine hundred attendees at the 2023 TGIA Annual Conference, I drew a connection between David Duke and Donald Trump. I expected at best a cold reception.

For the majority opinion in the 1857 US Supreme Court ruling in the infamous Dred Scott runaway slave case, Chief Justice Roger Taney wrote, "A black man had no rights that a white man is bound to respect...We think they are not [men], and that they were not included, and were not intended to be included under the word 'citizens' in the Constitution, and can therefore claim none of the rights and privileges of the United States..."

One hundred sixty-nine years later Donald Trump would express this same belief in the doctrine of white privilege and supremacy. While president of the United States, he would refer to African nations, Haiti, and El Salvador as "shithole countries." Then, refusing to vacate the White House despite losing both the electoral and the popular vote and waiting to unleash his January 6 coup d'état on American democracy, Trump ardently displayed his plantation master attitude by referring to his Black supporters as "*my* African Americans." He called Black Lives Matter and its attendant network a hate group for pursuing justice for the plethora of unarmed Black citizens victimized by the police. Yet on January 6, 2021, former militia and present white supremacist police officers almost overthrew the US government to stop the certification of President-Elect Joe Biden as the next commander in chief.

Even though the Supreme Court upheld the legal concept of qualified immunity, which protects police from prosecution for almost all unwarranted behavior, individual states are now changing their laws to hold police more accountable for their violent actions. With pressure from the electorate, the federal government and state legislators can continue to take incremental steps to revise unjust rules regarding policing. In addition to qualified immunity, there are other reforms that can yield the greatest amount of progress.

While the family of George Floyd was awarded a $27 million settlement for Floyd's wrongful death before Officer Derek Chauvin underwent his criminal trial—the largest civil settlement in such a case in US history—this will not foster police accountability; as Miriam Krinsky of Fair and Just Prosecution makes clear, taxpayers not police unions will pay the settlement. Nor has it been determined yet how the Minneapolis Police Department will receive better training to curtail the use of deadly force. In the last ten years, New York, Los Angeles, and Chicago have paid an astronomical $2.5 billion to settle misconduct lawsuits from a much-needed tax base rather than the coffers of police unions. As more cities become cash-poor, there is an incentive and opportunity to shift policing so that personnel with specialized psychological training can respond to unarmed assailants instead of police officers.

Legal precedents established in major police departments can inevitably lead to court cases in which the financial responsibility for excessive force violations is returned to police unions rather than already besieged taxpayers.

With over eighteen thousand individual police departments, municipalities, and jurisdictions in the United States, the confluence of underfunded and undertrained police and the tight bond between police unions and prosecutors' offices makes sweeping social justice changes to law enforcement policies and practices a cruelly daunting task. However, as Attorney General Merrick Garland's Department of Justice has already proven, federal guidelines for choke holds and use of force can curb police malfeasance at certain major regional departments. The same holds for federal pressure to utilize body cameras and enact no-knock exceptions. After the shooting death of Breonna Taylor during a disastrous raid in Kentucky, three states to date have banned the latter.

Despite the objections of New York City police unions, on March 4, 2021, more than eighty-three thousand current and former disciplinary records of NYPD officers were made available online. As more police departments make these records accessible—voluntarily or not—a national database of Brady lists can be configured to prevent the transferring or rehiring of unsuitable police officers.

The Pentagon's 1033 program must end. Through this program, the US Department of Defense provides excess equipment to participating agencies at no cost and little restriction. As the events in the aftermath of the killing of Michael Brown in Ferguson, Missouri, showed, the result is the irresponsible and destructive provision of military-grade equipment to police departments enforcing neighborhoods populated by people of color. Restrictions on existing use of military weaponry by law enforcement agencies must also be addressed on a case-by-case basis.

Despite the exasperatingly slow progress of police reform, it is essential to acknowledge that it is moving. States like Arkansas, Massachusetts, and Colorado have passed measures that require law enforcement officers to intercede when another officer is using excessive force. One test case in which officers, faced with criminal charges, testify against more culpable officers like Derek Chauvin could in effect change the interdepartmental relationships among the police union, mayor, rank-and-file officers, and, very significantly, the office of a district attorney.

Because prosecutors in major American cities may well hold the key to breakthroughs in police accountability, voters must overlook endorsements from police unions or law enforcement leaders when vetting potential candidates. Prosecutors must be able to independently investigate and prosecute officer-involved incidents and fatalities. Furthermore, an independent unit not beholden to the employing law enforcement agency should consult with the state's attorney general or independent prosecutor regarding any decision not to file criminal charges.

Another threat to civilians is the number of current and former police, military, and militia present at the Capitol

insurrection on January 6, 2021. According to the Brennan
Center for Justice, the Plain View Project has documented no
less than five thousand bigoted social media posts by thirty-five
hundred former and current police officers since 2019. Just as
cross-generational and multinational indignation rose up after
the slow-motion murder of George Floyd, so too did the friends
and relatives of those who would have overthrown the United
States government that day determine to turn in those traitors.
Those Americans who chose law and order and the continu-
ation of democracy over lies and unverified conspiracies are
patriots beyond measure. If we support them to combat racism, to continue the fight for free and fair elections, to help this
world survive a catastrophic pandemic and end unacceptable
congressional selfishness, our legacy will be the greatest democratic experiment the world has ever known.

The very future of democracy is imperiled right now as in
no other moment since the Civil War. During an international
pandemic, a majority of Republican legislators, unwilling to
help recover a devastated economy, simultaneously perpetu-
ated the lie that Trump won the 2020 election. Since biparti-
sanship in Congress is a relic of the past, it is crucial that every
facet of activist society—voter registrars, social justice organizations, and, where this book began, performing artists—prepare
for and commit more deeply to the battle for human rights.

With its huge, worldwide audience, hip-hop music must
maintain its validity as a form of protest. Issues of qualified
immunity, use of force, police body cameras, and more are just
as immediate and worthy of discussion as those raised by NWA

and Public Enemy when gangsta rap came into its own in the 1990s. With more than three hundred pieces of legislation primarily in southern states seeking to limit access to voting for people of color in retribution for the electoral achievements of the Democratic Party, we need all the popular artists in every succeeding generation we can muster.

In my talks about gangsta rap, I do not repeat lyrics but perform them the way they are meant to be experienced. I began my presentation at the TGIA 2023 conference with "Ya Want Sum a Dis?" by South Central Cartel, who are Crips. "How many of you think that's a gangsta rap song?" Half of the nine hundred participants raised their hands. "It's actually an anti-gang song. Really listen to what they're saying. *You want some of this*—meaning gangs—*you're a stupid motherfucker.*" I saw the lightbulbs going off and heads nodding. "That's what gangsta rap is about. You have to take the time to listen to what is actually being said and to put it into context. In this case, the lyrics *some of this* are anti-gang, about not getting in the game.

"Look, the gangsta rap I'm talking to you about is over thirty years old," I continued in my talk. "I don't keep up with it like I used to because quite frankly I think the gangster rap of today—or what they might call gangster rap today—is a bunch of crap. If you want to understand this music, go back to the beginning. Go back to Ice Cube, NWA, South Central Cartel, DJ Quik…These guys fashioned this format, and they put out what I consider to be good music. It just has a gangster theme to it. You need to understand it from that perspective."

At the point in my lecture when I discussed the Black

Klansman investigation, I described my conversations over the phone with David Duke, specifically how he liked to be fawned over and how by complimenting him I drew more out of him. "In many respects," I said, "he's like Donald Trump." And as I said this, I looked at different segments of the audience. From the Black folks, I got the affirmative head nods. Everyone else gave me those nervous stares, and I knew they didn't like the comparison. But I didn't give a shit.

My audience at the conference was a new generation of police officers. Some of the attendees knew my work well, being close to my age or having been in police work for thirty, forty years. But most of them were young cops who had heard only of my reputation. I felt honored to be described as the god-father of gang cops, a mentor to my peers all over the country for over thirty years, especially because I feel that designation belongs to those in the LAPD who were the first to confront the problem and shared their knowledge and experience with their peers throughout the country. "Show respect for him," said an officer from Dallas. "Pay proper respect to him for what he went through and what he did to make it better for all of us." Then he stood up, and the conference attendees gave me the second standing ovation of my career. I started to cry like a baby.

But the recognition did not end there. After my presentation, attendees approached me individually. Because of *BlacKkKlansman*, people perceive me as a minor celebrity, and I have come to expect them to request my autograph and a photograph with me. I asked how long they had been cops, and many would answer only three to five years. That means they were in diapers when I retired from police work. Since they were not around during my heyday, they had only heard about my presentations and did not believe that I could rap the songs that I referenced. These young cops were fascinated when in the midst of my talk, I broke out with "Crooked Officer" by the Geto Boys and NWA's "Fuck tha Police."

"This lived up to everything we heard," they said. "We appreciate it. We appreciate you."

At one point, I had to sit down because of issues with my leg. Only then did I look behind me and notice the line of attendees to have a photograph taken with me. It extended halfway across the room, and the sight of it made me emotional again.

Then came the ultimate honor. If you are familiar with military culture, you may know about the significance of challenge coins. Each branch of the military has a medallion with its distinct insignia and motto that it gives to members of exemplary achievements and service. Many entities such as police forces and fire departments have adopted the military tradition of awarding challenge coins, and they are selective. To receive a challenge coin from your unit is a major honor in and of itself. It is also a high distinction for someone to give a challenge coin bestowed upon them by their organization to someone else who is not a member. It is a symbol of a colleague's acknowledgment of and appreciation for the significant contributions you have made to their profession or organization. Let's say you are at a bar, and someone gives you their challenge coin. The tradition calls for you to offer your own challenge coin to them. The two of you exchange coins, have a drink together, and become comrades.

I left the 2023 Annual Conference of the Texas Gang Investigators Association with twenty challenge coins. In fact, the last one I received was the day before I left. Explaining that he did not have a chance to stand in line to give me his challenge coin, a cop presented it to me in the hotel lobby.

My ultimate message to law enforcement about the relevance of gangsta rap and its offshoots remains the same: We must recognize the music as a tool to make us better cops. Cops must listen to the songs, and if you fail to do so, shame on you. The rappers are not making a definitive statement against the police. They're talking about negative aspects of social conditions in which they exist, and which you are a part of. You do not have to agree with their thinking, but you simply must understand it. My philosophy has always been to try to make the community I serve a little better, and if I can do that by getting into the heads of the kids who are on the streets of the community as gangsters, then that makes me a better cop and a better human being.

And that's what we should all strive for.

AFTERWORD

by Dr. William A. Smith, Professor of Ethnic Studies,
Chair, Department of Education, Culture and Society,
University of Utah

All domination is, in the last instance, maintained through social control strategies," wrote noted Afro Puerto Rican sociologist Eduardo Bonilla-Silva in his seminal book *White Supremacy and Racism in the Post–Civil Rights Era.* He described the highly repressive as well as paternalistic practices used to keep Blacks in their place: the whips and night patrols of slavery, and the strict, unwritten rules of Jim Crow that followed abolition, with lynching and other terroristic forms of social control used as insurance to specify that place "of [B]lacks in the new environment of 'freedom' and safeguard white supremacy. As Jim Crow practices subsided," wrote Professor Bonilla-Silva, "the control of [B]lacks is today chiefly attained through state agencies (e.g., the police, the criminal court system, and the FBI)."

He is speaking of a historical moment that manifests in current conditions, and there have been many freedom fighters—known and unknown—who have risen to the call of humanity to fight against racial and social injustices. Many of these people were part of an organization that supported and protected them. However, this book is about one hip-hop freedom fighter, Ron Stallworth, who often found himself as the only Black man fighting for an organized group within conservative police departments and in meetings with right-leaning religious leaders and government officials.

I study the traumatic effects of racism and stress, and my research is on racial battle fatigue (systemic-racism-related repetitive stress injury), a concept I coined in 2003. I first met Ron around 2001–02 when we worked together on several state-level committees centered on rectifying problematic laws and law enforcement practices that racially minoritized communities faced. I did not know about Ron's first life as an undercover Black Klansman, and I was amazed by his resilience as a Black police officer despite the racism that he has experienced. Moreover, I was drawn to him because of his resilience to mitigate racial battle fatigue while working in law enforcement around racially conservative and often racist people.

Ron and I sat next to each other in many of our committee meetings, but since he was a cop, I accepted him cautiously at first. He proved that he never lost his pro-Black consciousness of what "the people" were dealing with and maintained a "Power to the People" ideology, and my appreciation organically grew based on his honesty and willingness to speak up in these meetings and share strategies from this "hip-hop cop" framework. Still, I was surprised to learn in a 2006 newspaper interview of Ron's first significant career sacrifice, and I am overwhelmed that he has penned his second book because in *The Gangs of Zion*, we meet the Ron Stallworth that I grew to know and appreciate.

In his latest memoir, Sergeant Ron Stallworth has created the first comprehensive examination of how a social justice hip-hop cop battles against the impenetrable "thin blue line" while constantly maintaining his Blackness. It tells of the sinister effects of fighting against gang life, illegal drugs, conservative politics and politicians, and stereotypical beliefs about gangsta rap and Black people. *The Gangs of Zion* adds more intimacy to Ron Stallworth's life than his 2014 memoir *Black Klansman*. "Kato," as he was known as a youth (based upon his commitment to the martial arts and the character Bruce Lee played in the 1960s television series *The Green Hornet*), has been fighting against bullies his entire life. As an adult, as Officer Stallworth, he continued a fight for truth and justice that took him from city mayors' offices to multiple appearances before the House Judiciary Committee's Subcommittee on Crime. As a Black man and law enforcer, Stallworth offers a fresh, complex account of the strengths and challenges of gangsta rap, hip-hop, Black life, and what law enforcement must become for all people. No memoir in recent history has offered me this much perspective with no holds barred. I am glad that my friend has provided us with another significant glimpse into his life in a manner that can be discussed in book clubs, secondary education classrooms, and both undergraduate and graduate social science courses.

The famous American scholar, historian, and sociologist Dr. W. E. B. Du Bois stated in his 1935 book *Black Reconstruction in America* that "nations reel and stagger on their way; they make hideous mistakes; they commit frightful wrongs; they do great and beautiful things. And shall we not best guide humanity by telling the truth about all this, so far as the truth is ascertainable?"

Fortunately for us, Ron Stallworth's truth has been shared with us in a manner that will help guide humanity from the lessons learned throughout his hip-hop cop career.

ACKNOWLEDGMENTS

First and foremost, I want to thank my wife, Patsy Terrazas Stallworth, for her technological help (I am computer illiterate). When I expressed frustration over an issue and was ready to throw the computer against the wall, she calmly took matters in her hands and found the solution to my frustration. As always, she has been my rock and kept me grounded. My love for her knows no bounds.

Second, thanks to Andy Frances, my business manager. Without his backing and support, I would not have experienced the honor and joy of becoming a *New York Times* bestselling author for my first memoir, *Black Klansman* (edited by James Melia). Andy's tireless effort ultimately led to my and Patsy's roller-coaster experience in Hollywood and the eventual Academy Award win for the movie adaptation of my book.

A hearty thank-you to Brad Schreiber for his input toward this project.

Finally, a special thank-you to my co-author, Sofia Quintero.

She steered this project to its finale. Her contributions have been invaluable.

A special consideration to Dr. William A. Smith, professor in the University of Utah's Department of Education, Culture and Society, for the kind words offered in the afterword.

Finally, special thanks to Ms. Celeste Fine of Park & Fine Literary agency. From the beginning of hearing this story, she championed its literary creation when others ignored it. I owe you a debt of gratitude.

—*Ron Stallworth*